JUMBLE®

Masterpiece

A Crowning Achievement of Puzzles!

T0206722

Henri Arnold,
Bob Lee,
Jeff Knurek, &
David L. Hoyt

TRIUMPH
BOOKS

This book is available in quantity at special discounts
for your group or organization.

For further information, con tact:
Triumph Books LLC
814 North Franklin Street
Chicago, Illinois 60610
Phone: (312) 337-0747
www.triumphbooks.com

Printed in U.S.A.

ISBN: 978-1-62937-916-6

Design by Sue Knopf

Contents

JUMBLE®
Masterpiece

Classic Puzzles

PUZZLE
1

JUMBLE®

Unscramble these four Jumbles, one letter to each square, to form four ordinary words.

UPYPP
INGEF
CLUNKO
HIGLES
I need courage
HOW TO MAKE DRACULA HAPPY.

Now arrange the circled letters to form the surprise answer, as suggested by the above cartoon.

Print answer here ◯◯◯◯ YOUR ◯◯◯◯ ◯◯

PUZZLE
2

JUMBLE®

Unscramble these four Jumbles, one letter to each square, to form four ordinary words.

HOBOT
TRAIE
WEREVS
NOOMIK
Oh, well—the pay is good
HE LIKED THE JOB, BUT HATED THIS.

Now arrange the circled letters to form the surprise answer, as suggested by the above cartoon.

Print answer here

PUZZLE
3

JUMBLE®

Unscramble these four Jumbles, one letter to each square, to form four ordinary words.

PURUS
ERECK
CATBUD
SWORDY
WHAT A PERSON WHO SPENDS TOO MUCH TIME STUDYING CERAMICS MIGHT END UP AS.
Now arrange the circled letters to form the surprise answer, as suggested by the above cartoon.
Print answer here A

PUZZLE
4

JUMBLE®

Unscramble these four Jumbles, one letter to each square, to form four ordinary words.

DYNAD
WILLT
CLAISO
REVOUD
CASINO
It's all over for me
WHAT A GAMBLING ADDICT USUALLY IS.
Now arrange the circled letters to form the surprise answer, as suggested by the above cartoon.
Print answer here
AT
WITH THE

PUZZLE
5

JUMBLE®

Unscramble these four Jumbles, one letter to each square, to form four ordinary words.

DONUP

UNEES

DOUSIT

SWILEY

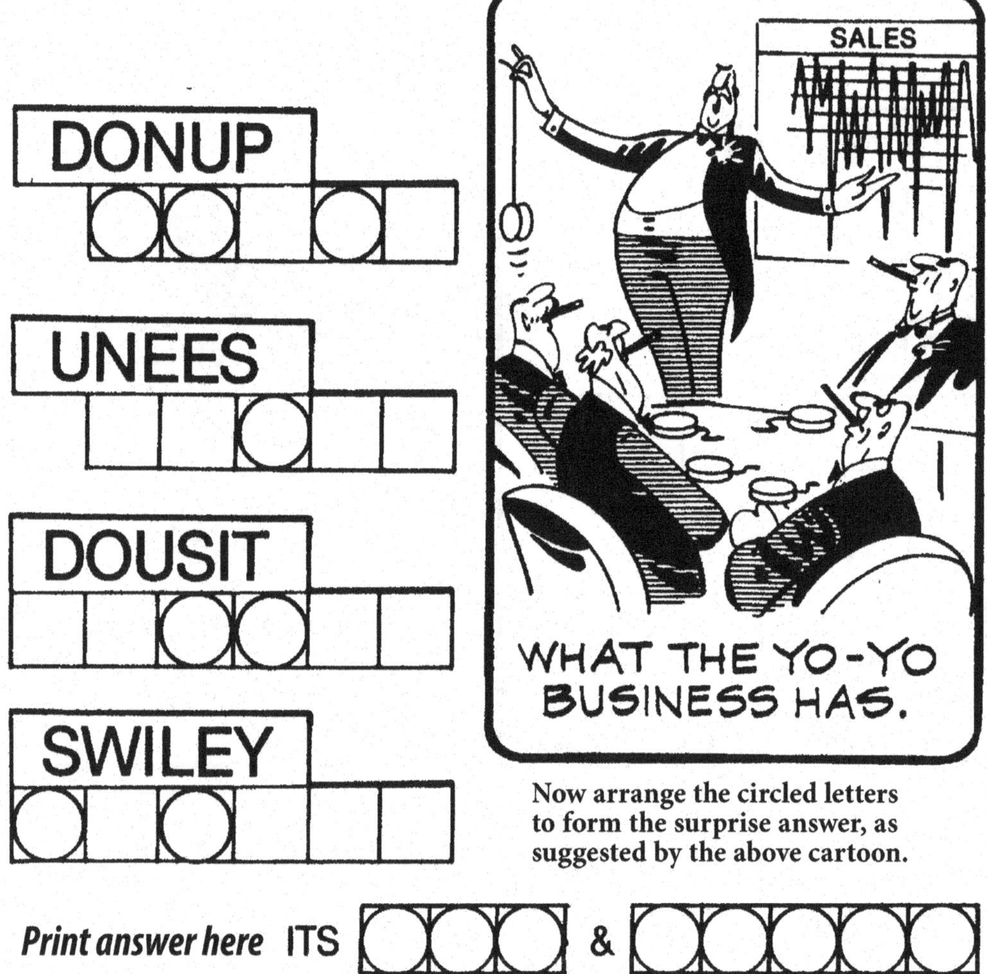
SALES
WHAT THE YO-YO BUSINESS HAS.

Now arrange the circled letters to form the surprise answer, as suggested by the above cartoon.

Print answer here ITS ◯◯◯ & ◯◯◯◯◯

PUZZLE
6

JUMBLE®

Unscramble these four Jumbles, one letter to each square, to form four ordinary words.

HANNE
MARRO
TOESGO
NOPPIL
ITALY
THAT CONCEITED GUY DIDN'T FEEL THE NEED FOR A VACATION BECAUSE HE WAS ALREADY ON THIS.

Now arrange the circled letters to form the surprise answer, as suggested by the above cartoon.

Print answer here

PUZZLE
7

JUMBLE®

Unscramble these four Jumbles, one letter to each square, to form four ordinary words.

RIMEN

CUDIL

SULTES

GELIGG

WHAT SHE SAID AT THE COSTUME PARTY.

Now arrange the circled letters to form the surprise answer, as suggested by the above cartoon.

Print answer here " - " FOR !

PUZZLE
8

JUMBLE®

Unscramble these four Jumbles, one letter to each square, to form four ordinary words.

VOCEL

HAGUL

WRAITE

ZALBER

A SPENDTHRIFT WIFE MIGHT LOVE HER HUSBAND FOR THIS.

Now arrange the circled letters to form the surprise answer, as suggested by the above cartoon.

Print answer here HE'S

PUZZLE
9

JUMBLE®

Unscramble these four Jumbles, one letter to each square, to form four ordinary words.

CIKHT
WREEF
STEBIC
STOLCY
Heh heh—I win the match!
HOW A HANDICAPPED GOLFER PLAYS.

Now arrange the circled letters to form the surprise answer, as suggested by the above cartoon.

Print answer here ◯◯◯◯ HIS ◯◯◯◯

PUZZLE
10

JUMBLE®

Unscramble these four Jumbles, one letter to each square, to form four ordinary words.

CADEY
DRAYT
COSHUL
LUPPER
WHAT AN EASY TALKER GENERALLY IS.
A

Now arrange the circled letters to form the surprise answer, as suggested by the above cartoon.

Print answer here

PUZZLE
11

JUMBLE®

Unscramble these four Jumbles, one letter to each square, to form four ordinary words.

RYTUL
KADEB
SEJERY
PLINEP
This'll wow 'em!
WHAT THE AUDIENCE GAVE HIM WHEN HE WAS EXPECTING CHEERS.

Now arrange the circled letters to form the surprise answer, as suggested by the above cartoon.

Print answer here

PUZZLE
12

JUMBLE®

Unscramble these four Jumbles, one letter to each square, to form four ordinary words.

IPEEC

TINFE

HERTHS

MIDOWS

WHAT A GOOD SHRINK IS SUPPOSED TO BE.

Now arrange the circled letters to form the surprise answer, as suggested by the above cartoon.

Print answer here A

PUZZLE
13

JUMBLE®

Unscramble these four Jumbles, one letter to each square, to form four ordinary words.

CAINP

GUDOH

DOLSUN

SARGYS

MGR
WHAT FORM OF SPEECH IS DOUBLE-TALK?

Now arrange the circled letters to form the surprise answer, as suggested by the above cartoon.

Print answer here VERY " "

PUZZLE
14

JUMBLE®

Unscramble these four Jumbles, one letter to each square, to form four ordinary words.

DYLOM
KAQUE
VEGASA
HECARB
WHAT THAT GIRL WHO LOOKED LIKE A MILLION BUCKS WAS.
Now arrange the circled letters to form the surprise answer, as suggested by the above cartoon.
Print answer here
JUST AS
TO

PUZZLE
15

JUMBLE®

Unscramble these four Jumbles, one letter to each square, to form four ordinary words.

AGGUE

RICLY

DUPHEL

MONFIR

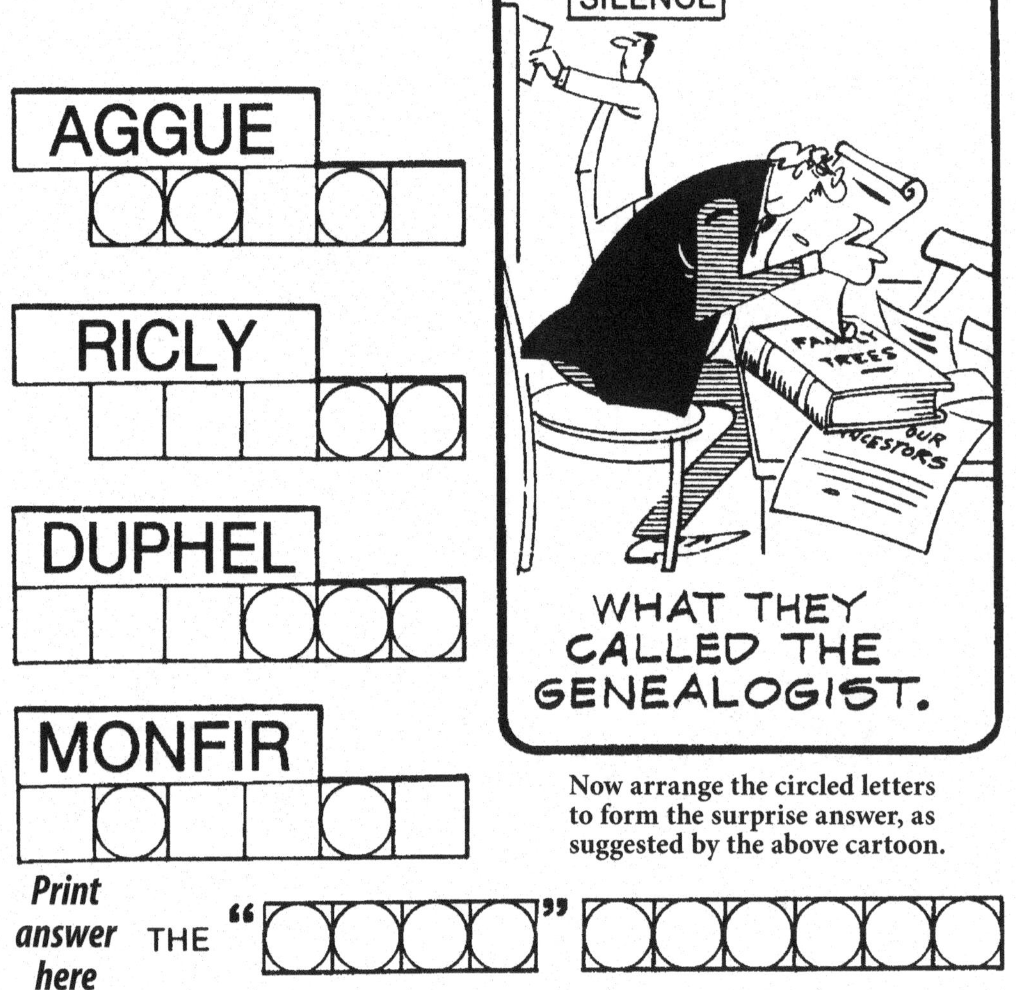
SILENCE
FAMILY TREES
OUR ANCESTORS
WHAT THEY CALLED THE GENEALOGIST.

Now arrange the circled letters to form the surprise answer, as suggested by the above cartoon.

Print answer here THE " "

PUZZLE
16

JUMBLE®

Unscramble these four Jumbles, one letter to each square, to form four ordinary words.

CAZER
NAREY
DILERB
TESHEE
Those were great times
WHAT NOSTALGIA SUMMONS UP.

Now arrange the circled letters to form the surprise answer, as suggested by the above cartoon.

Print answer here "◯◯◯◯◯◯-◯◯◯◯"

PUZZLE
17

JUMBLE®

Unscramble these four Jumbles, one letter to each square, to form four ordinary words.

EVING

TOAFO

NITTEK

YASILE

This is your idea of taking me out to dinner?
WHAT THEY CALLED THAT STINGY DERMATOLOGIST.

Now arrange the circled letters to form the surprise answer, as suggested by the above cartoon.

Print answer here A

PUZZLE
18

JUMBLE®

Unscramble these four Jumbles, one letter to each square, to form four ordinary words.

BREWO
FYTHE
ENDECT
DILPIM
Another one of your imaginary ailments?
WHAT A HYPOCHONDRIAC'S AFFLICTION FREQUENTLY IS.
A

Now arrange the circled letters to form the surprise answer, as suggested by the above cartoon.

Print answer here

PUZZLE
19

JUMBLE®

Unscramble these four Jumbles, one letter to each square, to form four ordinary words.

GAADE
SOUMY
NESTOL
BORCAN
WHAT HE SAID WHEN THE JUDGE SENTENCED HIM TO BE HANGED.
Print answer here
THAT'S " "

Now arrange the circled letters to form the surprise answer, as suggested by the above cartoon.

PUZZLE
20

JUMBLE®

Unscramble these four Jumbles, one letter to each square, to form four ordinary words.

FEASH
MAYOF
DINNAL
PENOLY
He's very conceited
WHAT THE EGOTISTICAL NUDIST WAS ALL WRAPPED UP IN.

Now arrange the circled letters to form the surprise answer, as suggested by the above cartoon.

Print answer here

PUZZLE
21

JUMBLE®

Unscramble these four Jumbles, one letter to each square, to form four ordinary words.

GLUBY
HALET
GLINJE
INDOWS
WHAT NOBILITY USUALLY IS.

Now arrange the circled letters to form the surprise answer, as suggested by the above cartoon.

Print answer here " ◯◯◯◯ - ◯◯◯◯◯ "

PUZZLE
22

JUMBLE®

Unscramble these four Jumbles, one letter to each square, to form four ordinary words.

SHECS
HIRMT
DREHWS
TIPIDE
WHAT A MINISKIRT IS.

Now arrange the circled letters to form the surprise answer, as suggested by the above cartoon.

Print answer here A "[ ][ ][ ][ ][ ] - [ ][ ][ ][ ][ ]"

PUZZLE
23

JUMBLE®

Unscramble these four Jumbles, one letter to each square, to form four ordinary words.

NUTED
RYGOL
ANGOLS
DEBUMI
HOW THAT PERFUME HELD HIM.
Now arrange the circled letters to form the surprise answer, as suggested by the above cartoon.
Print answer here
" - "

PUZZLE
24

JUMBLE®

Unscramble these four Jumbles, one letter to each square, to form four ordinary words.

CULOT
LAMBY
LESING
TREBUT
WHAT YOU NEED TO HAVE IN ORDER TO BE AN ORGAN GRINDER.

Now arrange the circled letters to form the surprise answer, as suggested by the above cartoon.

Print answer here A ◯◯◯◯ FOR ◯◯◯◯◯

PUZZLE
25

JUMBLE®

Unscramble these four Jumbles, one letter to each square, to form four ordinary words.

IKYTT
LAVEE
KABREY
GANTEM
WHERE THE OPERA SINGER'S LITTLE ARIA CAME FROM.

Now arrange the circled letters to form the surprise answer, as suggested by the above cartoon.

Print answer here ◯ ◯◯◯◯ "◯◯◯◯◯"

JUMBLE®
Masterpiece

Daily Puzzles

PUZZLE
26

JUMBLE®

Unscramble these four Jumbles, one letter to each square, to form four ordinary words.

BUTOD
KWONN
TEECIX
JAVILO
WHAT THE BUS DRIVER SAID.

Now arrange the circled letters to form the surprise answer, as suggested by the above cartoon.

Print answer here " ☐☐☐☐ " IN THE ☐☐☐!

PUZZLE
27

JUMBLE®

Unscramble these four Jumbles, one letter to each square, to form four ordinary words.

TACCH
GLINY
SIGUNE
VISNAH
WHAT THERE WAS PLENTY OF AT THAT PENTHOUSE.

Now arrange the circled letters to form the surprise answer, as suggested by the above cartoon.

Print answer here

PUZZLE
28

JUMBLE®

Unscramble these four Jumbles, one letter to each square, to form four ordinary words.

MEWNO
ENPAC
DEVAHL
TRUGET
YAK YAK
YAK YAK
WHAT THOSE TALKATIVE MOTHS DID.
Now arrange the circled letters to form the surprise answer, as suggested by the above cartoon.
Print answer here
THE

PUZZLE
29

JUMBLE®

Unscramble these four Jumbles, one letter to each square, to form four ordinary words.

GEWIH

NUBEG

TYLPEN

AURBUE

Boy—are you fat!
HOW SOME FRANK PEOPLE MAKE THEIR POINT.

Now arrange the circled letters to form the surprise answer, as suggested by the above cartoon.

Print answer here BY

PUZZLE
30

JUMBLE®

Unscramble these four Jumbles, one letter to each square, to form four ordinary words.

NAIRY

BUICT

ETOLAC

DULBOY

TIRED OF LOOKING AT ALL THOSE ROADSIDE ADS.

Now arrange the circled letters to form the surprise answer, as suggested by the above cartoon.

Print answer here " ____ - _____ "

PUZZLE
31

JUMBLE®

Unscramble these four Jumbles, one letter to each square, to form four ordinary words.

AKARP
CITOX
DYPSOR
CRADOC
WHAT A PERSON WHO SPENDS EVERY AFTERNOON WATCHING TV UNDOUBTEDLY IS.
Now arrange the circled letters to form the surprise answer, as suggested by the above cartoon.
Print answer here
A " "

PUZZLE
32

JUMBLE®

Unscramble these four Jumbles, one letter to each square, to form four ordinary words.

JABON
OVERP
EVIDID
THINEZ
WHAT THE HULA DANCER DID TO THE GUYS IN THE AUDIENCE.
Now arrange the circled letters to form the surprise answer, as suggested by the above cartoon.
Print answer here
" - " 'EM

PUZZLE
33

JUMBLE®

Unscramble these four Jumbles, one letter to each square, to form four ordinary words.

TILUQ

EGGOR

HANKES

LOUBES

WHY THEY ALWAYS ACCUSED HIM OF BEING NEGATIVE.

Now arrange the circled letters to form the surprise answer, as suggested by the above cartoon.

Print answer here HE WAS A "◯◯-◯◯-◯◯◯"

PUZZLE
34

JUMBLE®

Unscramble these four Jumbles, one letter to each square, to form four ordinary words.

GIMED

YUNTT

YORCAN

BLUESH

WHAT HER STEADY DATE WAS MUCH OF THE TIME.

Now arrange the circled letters to form the surprise answer, as suggested by the above cartoon.

Print answer here

PUZZLE
35

JUMBLE®

Unscramble these four Jumbles, one letter to each square, to form four ordinary words.

MOBIL
BLAWR
EURUFT
PHONTY
WHEN IT COMES TO A DISHWASHER, MOST EVERY HUSBAND WOULD RATHER DO THIS.
LOVE
Now arrange the circled letters to form the surprise answer, as suggested by the above cartoon.
Print answer here

PUZZLE
36

JUMBLE®

Unscramble these four Jumbles, one letter to each square, to form four ordinary words.

VOYCE

YIZZD

THINGK

DARZAH

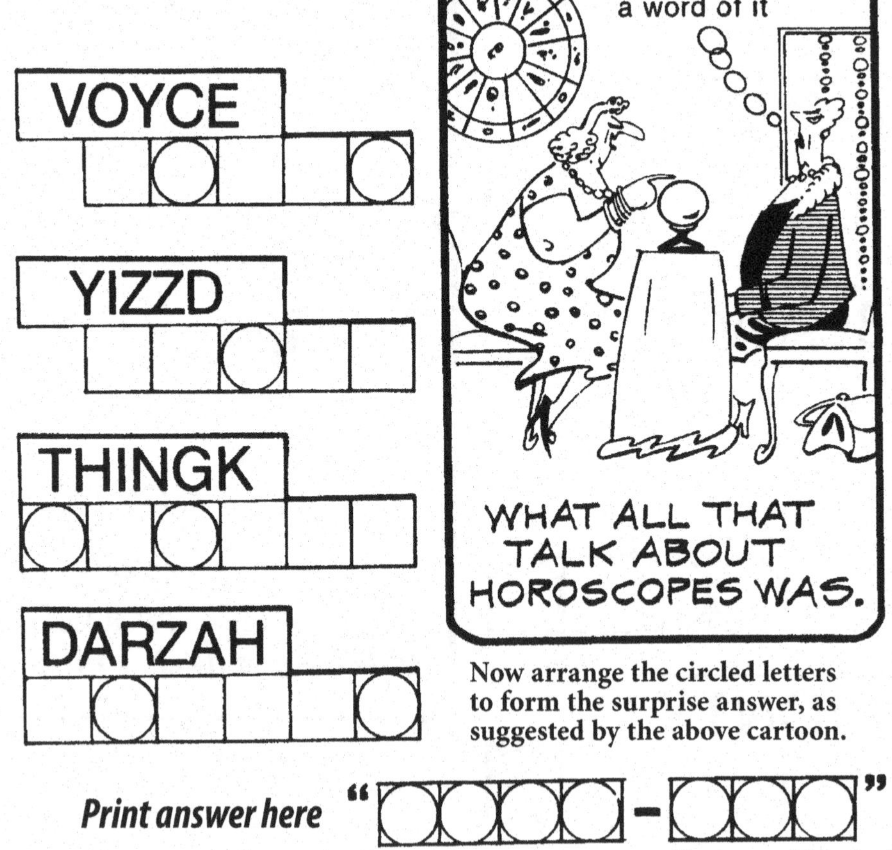
I don't believe a word of it
WHAT ALL THAT TALK ABOUT HOROSCOPES WAS.

Now arrange the circled letters to form the surprise answer, as suggested by the above cartoon.

Print answer here "[ ][ ][ ][ ][ ]-[ ][ ][ ]"

PUZZLE
37

JUMBLE®

Unscramble these four Jumbles, one letter to each square, to form four ordinary words.

CEMIN
LEXEP
MAINEA
DEWIST
I'm going out shopping
A COUNTERFEITER IS THE ONLY MAN IN THE WORLD WHO MAKES MORE MONEY THAN THIS.

Now arrange the circled letters to form the surprise answer, as suggested by the above cartoon.

Print answer here ANYONE

PUZZLE
38

JUMBLE®

Unscramble these four Jumbles, one letter to each square, to form four ordinary words.

WYSON
RYMEE
NATIED
TOGIER
WHAT THE GLOBE-
TROTTER HAD.
Now arrange the circled letters
to form the surprise answer, as
suggested by the above cartoon.
Print
answer
here
A " "

PUZZLE
39

JUMBLE®

Unscramble these four Jumbles, one letter to each square, to form four ordinary words.

IMECH
DANGL
FLANEL
REVABE
JEALOUSY SETS IN WITH THE ARRIVAL OF THIS.

Now arrange the circled letters to form the surprise answer, as suggested by the above cartoon.

Print answer here

PUZZLE
40

JUMBLE®

Unscramble these four Jumbles, one letter to each square, to form four ordinary words.

RUCRY
SOUPI
CEADDE
TUSALE
Hello. . .
Insurance
company?
HOW CARELESS DRIVERS FREQUENTLY END UP.

Now arrange the circled letters to form the surprise answer, as suggested by the above cartoon.

Print answer here " "

PUZZLE
41

JUMBLE®

Unscramble these four Jumbles, one letter to each square, to form four ordinary words.

MENOG
KASHY
SACULE
CEITED
As I always said, he's got a great future
THE "GO-GETTER" KNOWS THAT THE RULES FOR GETTING AHEAD WON'T WORK UNLESS THIS HAPPENS.

Now arrange the circled letters to form the surprise answer, as suggested by the above cartoon.

Print answer here

PUZZLE
42

JUMBLE®

Unscramble these four Jumbles, one letter to each square, to form four ordinary words.

CHABT
TALEE
EUGLED
FEWURC
He's sure gone far
WHAT THAT "GO-GETTER" FINALLY MANAGED TO DO.

Now arrange the circled letters to form the surprise answer, as suggested by the above cartoon.

Print answer here " " "

PUZZLE
43

JUMBLE®

Unscramble these four Jumbles, one letter to each square, to form four ordinary words.

YORIN
GERAW
DEBOHL
RAFAIN
WHAT ACCORDION MUSIC MIGHT SOMETIMES BE.

Now arrange the circled letters to form the surprise answer, as suggested by the above cartoon.

Print answer here OUT

PUZZLE
44

JUMBLE®

Unscramble these four Jumbles, one letter to each square, to form four ordinary words.

DANAP
RIMON
YENKOD
CREEFI
WHERE CAN YOU BUY CAMEL'S MILK?
Tee hee

Now arrange the circled letters to form the surprise answer, as suggested by the above cartoon.

Print answer here AT A "◯◯◯◯◯-◯◯◯◯◯"

PUZZLE
45

JUMBLE®

Unscramble these four Jumbles, one letter to each square, to form four ordinary words.

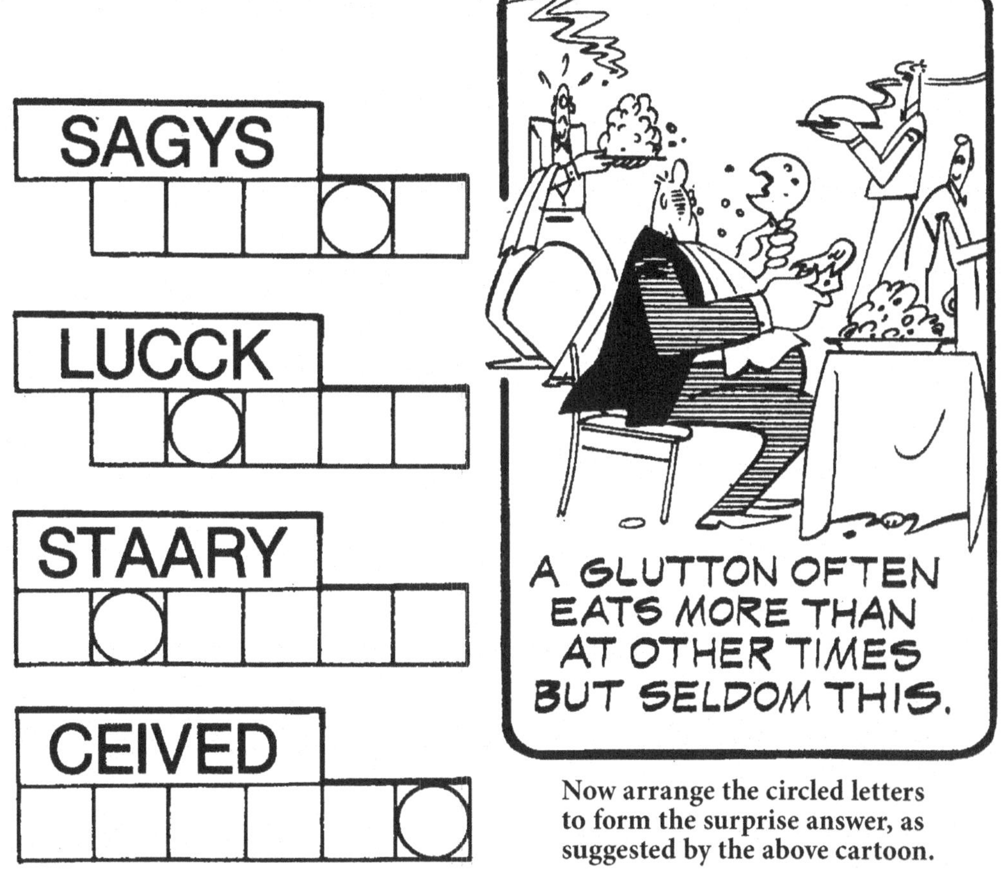
SAGYS
LUCCK
STAARY
CEIVED
A GLUTTON OFTEN EATS MORE THAN AT OTHER TIMES BUT SELDOM THIS.

Now arrange the circled letters to form the surprise answer, as suggested by the above cartoon.

Print answer here 

PUZZLE
46

JUMBLE®

Unscramble these four Jumbles, one letter to each square, to form four ordinary words.

SNAPY

MYDUP

RUGLAF

KOJECY

That's what I get for going on a blind date
WHAT SHE SAID ABOUT THAT DISAPPOINTING LETTER CARRIER.

Now arrange the circled letters to form the surprise answer, as suggested by the above cartoon.

Print answer here ◯◯◯◯ "◯◯◯◯◯"!

PUZZLE
47

JUMBLE®

Unscramble these four Jumbles, one letter to each square, to form four ordinary words.

TUQES
GYKAW
TOENED
RELUSY
WHAT TO WEAR WHEN WORKING OUTDOORS.
Now arrange the circled letters to form the surprise answer, as suggested by the above cartoon.
Print answer here
A “ ”

PUZZLE
48

JUMBLE®

Unscramble these four Jumbles, one letter to each square, to form four ordinary words.

PODEK

NOOHR

GLUTLE

SHMAIF

NES
WHAT A VISITOR TO HAWAII IS INTERESTED IN FINDING OUT ABOUT FIRST.

Now arrange the circled letters to form the surprise answer, as suggested by the above cartoon.

Print answer here THE "◯◯◯" OF THE ◯◯◯◯

PUZZLE
49

JUMBLE®

Unscramble these four Jumbles, one letter to each square, to form four ordinary words.

EGBIE
YONPE
DUSSIC
GREFOT
WHAT A MURKY FOG GIVES DRIVERS.
Now arrange the circled letters to form the surprise answer, as suggested by the above cartoon.
Print answer here THE " "

PUZZLE
50

JUMBLE®

Unscramble these four Jumbles, one letter to each square, to form four ordinary words.

NEQUE
AFTEC
KRILLE
PELPIN
Your new office, son
VICE-
PRESIDENT
WHAT NEPOTISM IS.

Now arrange the circled letters to form the surprise answer, as suggested by the above cartoon.

Print answer here " - "

PUZZLE
51

JUMBLE®

Unscramble these four Jumbles, one letter to each square, to form four ordinary words.

VANKE
WUNDE
UNJORI
BLOWEB
Sick—won't be in
WHAT AN ARTIST'S MODEL DOESN'T ALWAYS FEEL.

Now arrange the circled letters to form the surprise answer, as suggested by the above cartoon.

Print answer here IN THE "◯◯◯◯" FOR ◯◯◯◯

PUZZLE
52

JUMBLE®

Unscramble these four Jumbles, one letter to each square, to form four ordinary words.

REZIP

YALLD

YELLIK

NOWWIN

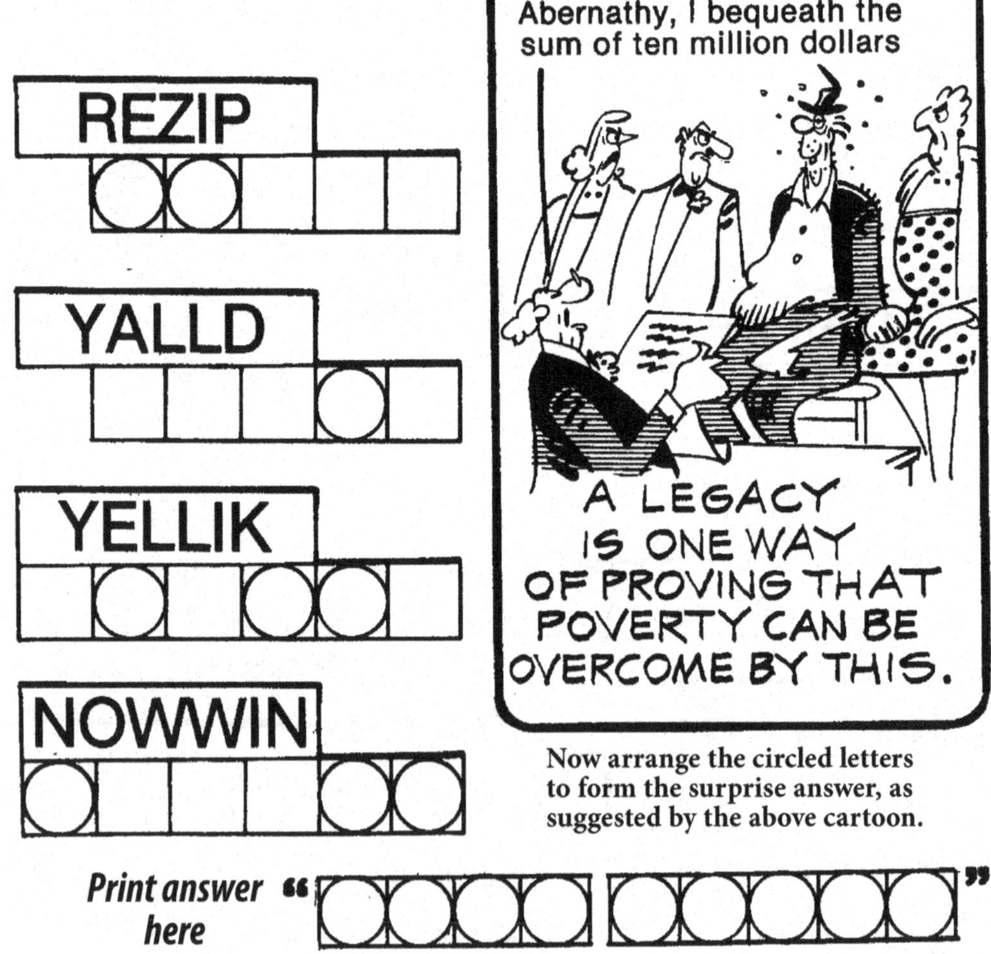
To my beloved cousin Abernathy, I bequeath the sum of ten million dollars
A LEGACY IS ONE WAY OF PROVING THAT POVERTY CAN BE OVERCOME BY THIS.

Now arrange the circled letters to form the surprise answer, as suggested by the above cartoon.

Print answer here " "

PUZZLE
53

JUMBLE®

Unscramble these four Jumbles, one letter to each square, to form four ordinary words.

FAHFC
DUESE
RITHEM
GLUNOE
She hit the ceiling with that one
WHAT THE SOPRANO'S "SOLO" WAS.

Now arrange the circled letters to form the surprise answer, as suggested by the above cartoon.

Print answer here

PUZZLE
54

JUMBLE®

Unscramble these four Jumbles, one letter to each square, to form four ordinary words.

POCUE
FROOG
TENNIT
CLOTEK
ALWAYS THE CENTER OF ATTENTION.

Now arrange the circled letters to form the surprise answer, as suggested by the above cartoon.

Print answer here THE

PUZZLE
55

JUMBLE®

Unscramble these four Jumbles, one letter to each square, to form four ordinary words.

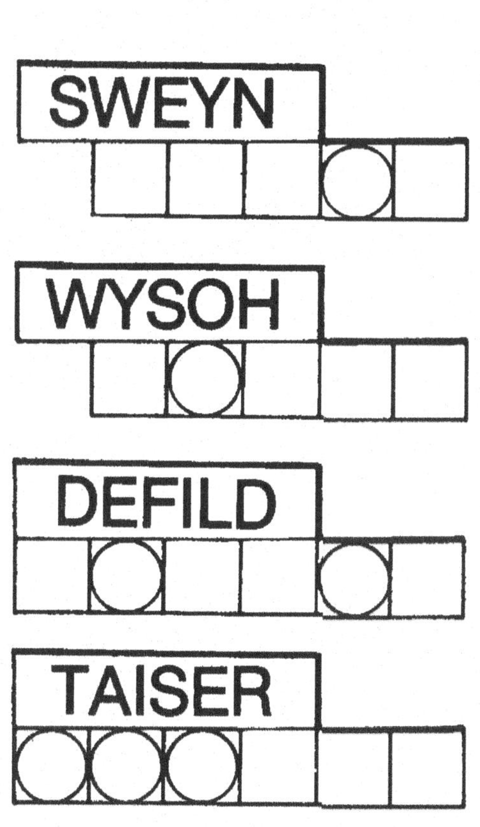
SWEYN
WYSOH
DEFILD
TAISER

May I call you Rodney?
SHE BEGAN TO CALL HIM BY HIS FIRST NAME WHEN SHE WAS AFTER THIS.

Now arrange the circled letters to form the surprise answer, as suggested by the above cartoon.

Print answer here

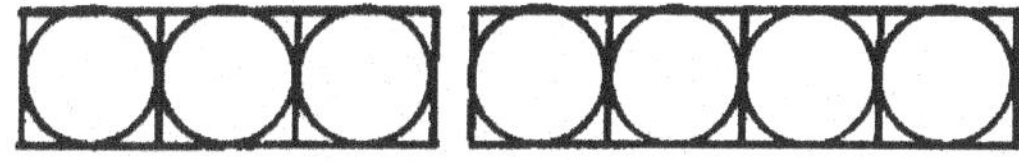

PUZZLE
56

JUMBLE®

Unscramble these four Jumbles, one letter to each square, to form four ordinary words.

SPAWM

GEELY

UPTYDE

NOOBBA

HELP WANTED
A LOAFER IS ALWAYS READY TO DO THIS, TO SAY THE LEAST.

Now arrange the circled letters to form the surprise answer, as suggested by the above cartoon.

Print answer here THE

PUZZLE
57

JUMBLE®

Unscramble these four Jumbles, one letter to each square, to form four ordinary words.

ENZOO
OBOAT
MILGRY
RUMIAD
THEY WERE PARTICIPANTS IN A SHOTGUN WEDDING.
Now arrange the circled letters to form the surprise answer, as suggested by the above cartoon.
Print answer here
THE
&
“ ”

PUZZLE
58

JUMBLE®

Unscramble these four Jumbles, one letter to each square, to form four ordinary words.

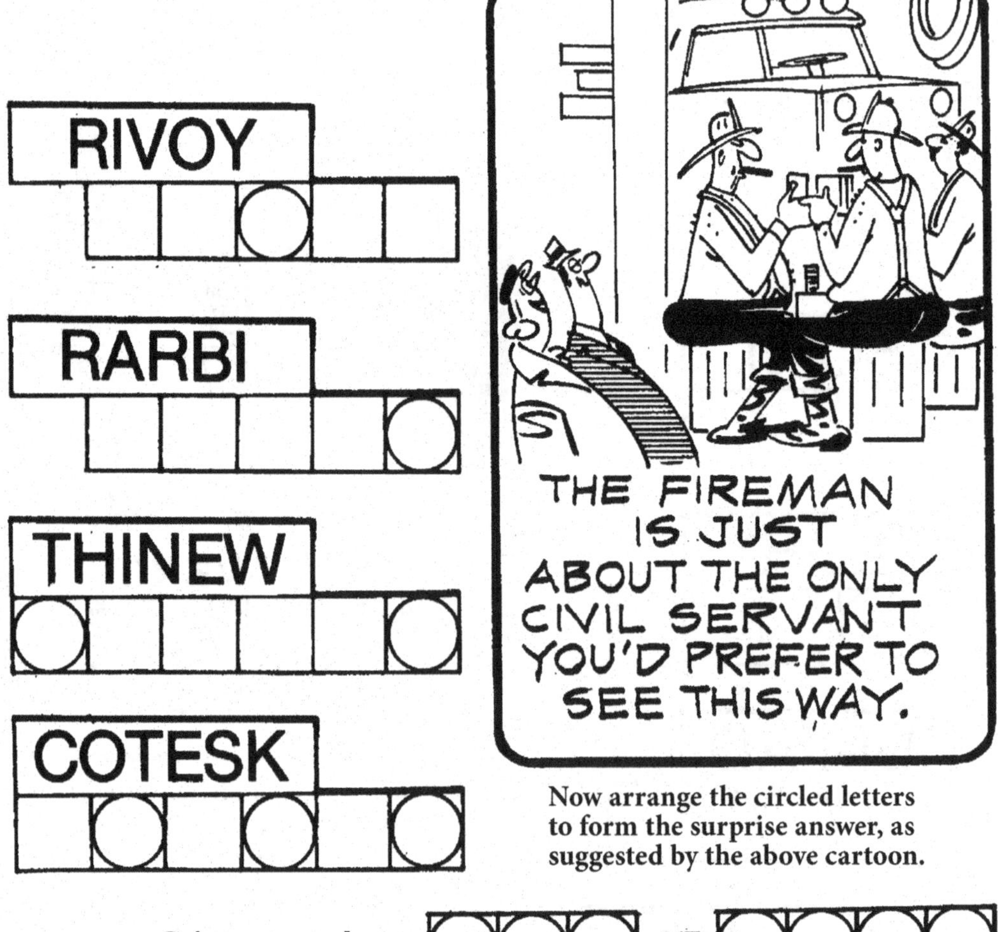
RIVOY
RARBI
THINEW
COTESK
THE FIREMAN IS JUST ABOUT THE ONLY CIVIL SERVANT YOU'D PREFER TO SEE THIS WAY.

Now arrange the circled letters to form the surprise answer, as suggested by the above cartoon.

Print answer here ☐☐☐ AT ☐☐☐☐

PUZZLE
59

JUMBLE®

Unscramble these four Jumbles, one letter to each square, to form four ordinary words.

NOONI
GOYGS
ALVASS
SWEENT
WHAT A PHILANDERER THINKS THE WORLD DOES.

Now arrange the circled letters to form the surprise answer, as suggested by the above cartoon.

Print answer here ◯◯◯◯ HIM A ◯◯◯◯◯◯

PUZZLE 60

JUMBLE®

Unscramble these four Jumbles, one letter to each square, to form four ordinary words.

NOYME

LOXET

FILTUP

ZIRDAL

THEY CALLED THE COMEDIAN A "GAS," BECAUSE HE WAS THIS.

Now arrange the circled letters to form the surprise answer, as suggested by the above cartoon.

Print answer here JUST AN ☐☐☐ "☐☐☐☐"

PUZZLE
61

JUMBLE®

Unscramble these four Jumbles, one letter to each square, to form four ordinary words.

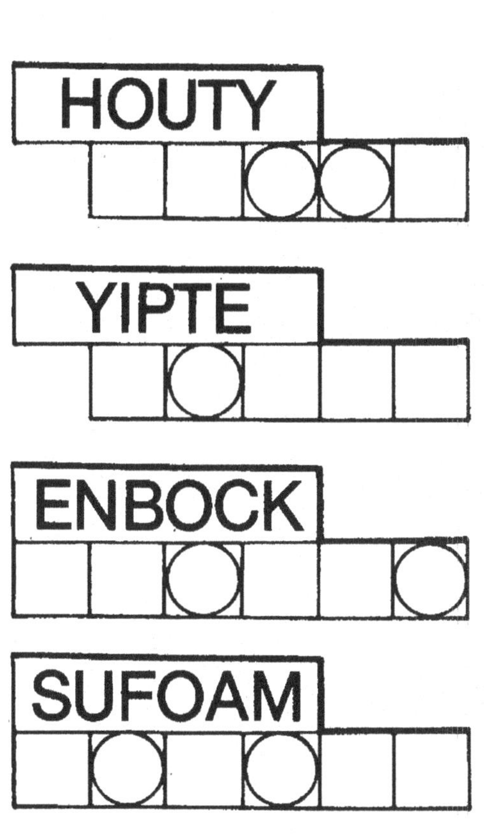
HOUTY
YIPTE
ENBOCK
SUFOAM

GYM

WHAT TO EXERCISE WHEN YOU FEEL YOU'RE PUTTING ON WEIGHT.

Now arrange the circled letters to form the surprise answer, as suggested by the above cartoon.

Print answer here

PUZZLE
62

JUMBLE®

Unscramble these four Jumbles, one letter to each square, to form four ordinary words.

MALGE
PRUPE
DISNAL
GITHEY
Never got a divorce
WHAT THAT TWICE-MARRIED SWINE COULD HAVE BEEN.

Now arrange the circled letters to form the surprise answer, as suggested by the above cartoon.

Print answer here A "___-_____"

PUZZLE
63

JUMBLE®

Unscramble these four Jumbles, one letter to each square, to form four ordinary words.

TRINP
MAITY
LEMAFE
DORIAH

I have a lovely table for you
TALKS WITHOUT GIVING ITSELF AWAY.

Now arrange the circled letters to form the surprise answer, as suggested by the above cartoon.

Print answer here

PUZZLE
64

JUMBLE®

Unscramble these four Jumbles, one letter to each square, to form four ordinary words.

TREXE
TCHEF
LAWTUN
RAHLED
TAXI
$
WHAT A
RAINY DAY IS
FOR A CABDRIVER.
Print answer here

Now arrange the circled letters to form the surprise answer, as suggested by the above cartoon.

PUZZLE
65

JUMBLE®

Unscramble these four Jumbles, one letter to each square, to form four ordinary words.

HASQU

BARRO

YAGTIE

CLETOH

I told you not to annoy the animals!
WHAT THE ZOOKEEPER SAID HIS LIFE WAS.

Now arrange the circled letters to form the surprise answer, as suggested by the above cartoon.

Print answer here " "

PUZZLE
66

JUMBLE®

Unscramble these four Jumbles, one letter to each square, to form four ordinary words.

DESTE
ODARR
CARECS
SHILER
WHAT SAMSON WAS AFTER DELILAH CUT OFF ALL HIS HAIR.

Now arrange the circled letters to form the surprise answer, as suggested by the above cartoon.

Print answer here " - "

PUZZLE
67

JUMBLE®

Unscramble these four Jumbles, one letter to each square, to form four ordinary words.

RACCK
YADDD
TIMLEG
SHOIBY
IRS
WHAT THE TAX COLLECTOR DID FOR THE MAN WHO THOUGHT HE WAS SAVING UP FOR A RAINY DAY.
Now arrange the circled letters to form the surprise answer, as suggested by the above cartoon.
Print answer here
“ ”

PUZZLE
68

JUMBLE®

Unscramble these four Jumbles, one letter to each square, to form four ordinary words.

EXIDO
GLUNE
VERYUP
CLARIA
WHAT MILK IS
FOR A CAT.

Now arrange the circled letters to form the surprise answer, as suggested by the above cartoon.

Print answer here THE "   " OF

PUZZLE
69

JUMBLE®

Unscramble these four Jumbles, one letter to each square, to form four ordinary words.

RODOP

DOREL

EUMMUS

CELLOA

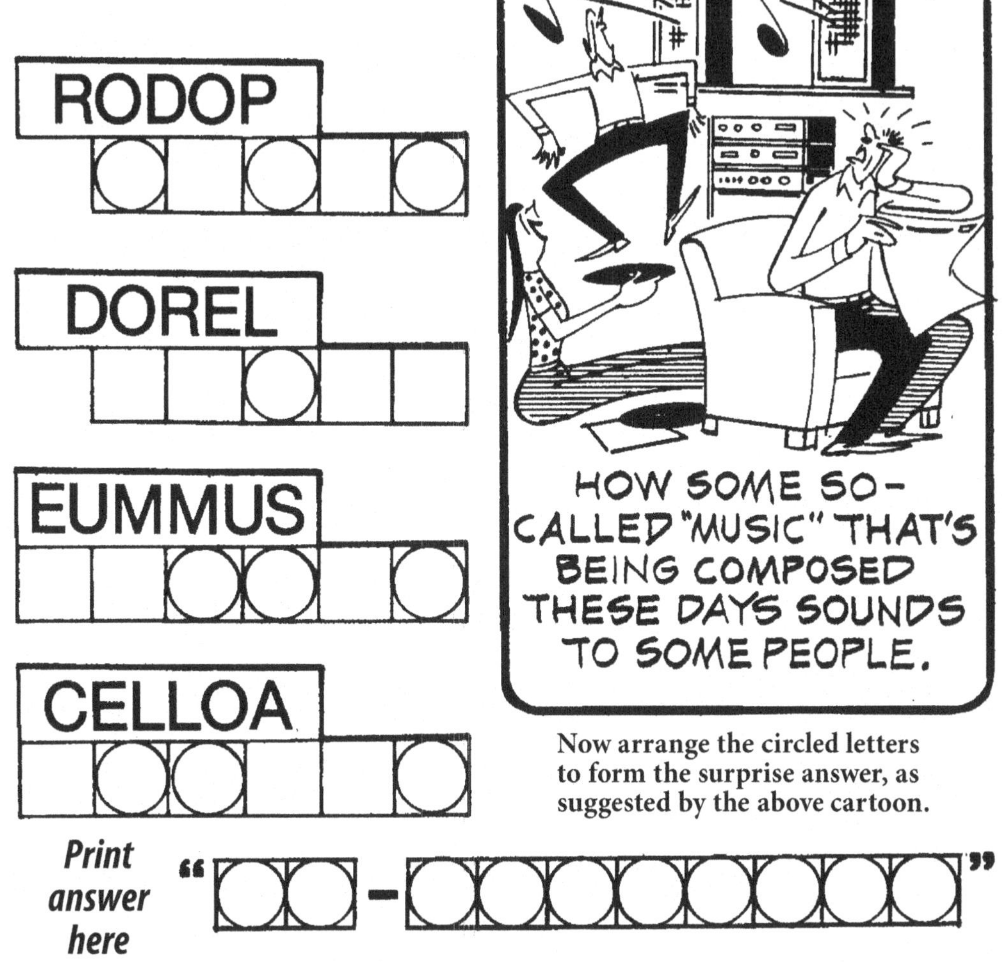
HOW SOME SO-CALLED "MUSIC" THAT'S BEING COMPOSED THESE DAYS SOUNDS TO SOME PEOPLE.

Now arrange the circled letters to form the surprise answer, as suggested by the above cartoon.

Print answer here "◯◯-◯◯◯◯◯◯◯◯"

PUZZLE
70

JUMBLE®

Unscramble these four Jumbles, one letter to each square, to form four ordinary words.

VARBE

PARPE

HARKEW

TAFOHM

WHAT HIS WIFE'S MOM TURNED OUT TO BE.

Now arrange the circled letters to form the surprise answer, as suggested by the above cartoon.

Print answer here A "▢▢▢▢▢▢ -IN- ▢▢▢"

PUZZLE
71

JUMBLE®

Unscramble these four Jumbles, one letter to each square, to form four ordinary words.

RYTAR
EDGUF
NIPPEG
ARROMT
Who would have thought?
THAT BACTERIOLOGIST MADE HIS FAMOUS DISCOVERY BY STARTING OUT WITH THIS.
Now arrange the circled letters to form the surprise answer, as suggested by the above cartoon.
Print answer here
THE
OF AN

PUZZLE
72

JUMBLE®

Unscramble these four Jumbles, one letter to each square, to form four ordinary words.

ORRUJ
ARING
LETTEK
CHECIT
DING
DONG
A GIRL WEARS A GIRDLE TO TAKE HER IN SO THAT A MAN WILL DO THIS.

Now arrange the circled letters to form the surprise answer, as suggested by the above cartoon.

Print answer here

PUZZLE
73

JUMBLE®

Unscramble these four Jumbles, one letter to each square, to form four ordinary words.

VATLE
TYDIT
INBOUN
NUCHEQ
WHAT HE DID AFTER STEALING A PAIR OF SCISSORS.

Now arrange the circled letters to form the surprise answer, as suggested by the above cartoon.

Print answer here " ◯◯◯ ◯◯◯ "

PUZZLE
74

JUMBLE®

Unscramble these four Jumbles, one letter to each square, to form four ordinary words.

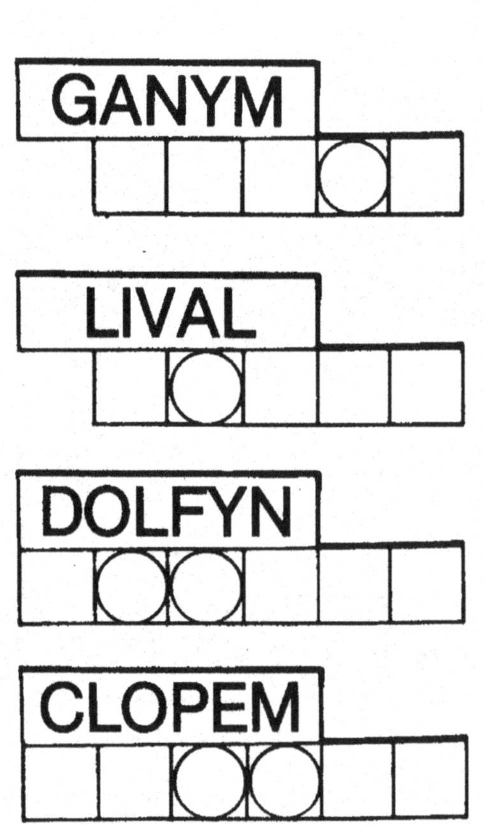

GANYM
LIVAL
DOLFYN
CLOPEM

He'll never get anywhere with that attitude!
A GUY WHO'S BUSY COPING HAS NO TIME FOR THIS.

Now arrange the circled letters to form the surprise answer, as suggested by the above cartoon.

Print answer here

PUZZLE
75

JUMBLE®

Unscramble these four Jumbles, one letter to each square, to form four ordinary words.

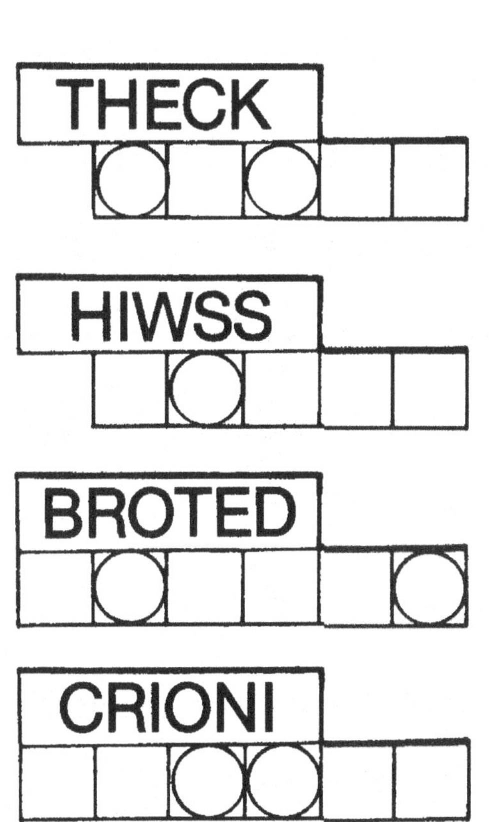
THECK
HIWSS
BROTED
CRIONI

WHAT THE FISHERMAN TURNED TV EXECUTIVE KNEW HOW TO MAKE.

Now arrange the circled letters to form the surprise answer, as suggested by the above cartoon.

Print answer here THE "◯◯◯" ◯◯◯◯

PUZZLE
76

JUMBLE®

Unscramble these four Jumbles, one letter to each square, to form four ordinary words.

NOSOW
BATOU
ZEEMAC
SMAJET
WHAT THAT PRACTICAL JOKER HAD.

Now arrange the circled letters to form the surprise answer, as suggested by the above cartoon.

Print answer here A ◯◯◯◯ FOR ◯◯◯◯

PUZZLE
77

JUMBLE®

Unscramble these four Jumbles, one letter to each square, to form four ordinary words.

YINSH
COPHE
GILOOG
GANTOU
See you next summer
WITH THAT DEAD-BEAT, IT'S OFTEN A MATTER OF THIS.

Now arrange the circled letters to form the surprise answer, as suggested by the above cartoon.

Print answer here ◯◯◯◯◯ & ◯◯

PUZZLE
78

JUMBLE®

Unscramble these four Jumbles, one letter to each square, to form four ordinary words.

SHAMC
CROFE
PAMERC
NUTTAR
!
HE WAS HOPING TO GET HIS TRIM FIGURE BACK, BUT ACTUALLY HAD THIS.

Now arrange the circled letters to form the surprise answer, as suggested by the above cartoon.

Print answer here A

PUZZLE
79

JUMBLE®

Unscramble these four Jumbles, one letter to each square, to form four ordinary words.

TRAFE

MELIP

FUMINF

WENTIG

Hurray! No school!
He won't be in

WHAT A BLIZZARD MIGHT DO TO DAILY LIFE.

Now arrange the circled letters to form the surprise answer, as suggested by the above cartoon.

Print answer here " - " IT

PUZZLE
80

JUMBLE®

Unscramble these four Jumbles, one letter to each square, to form four ordinary words.

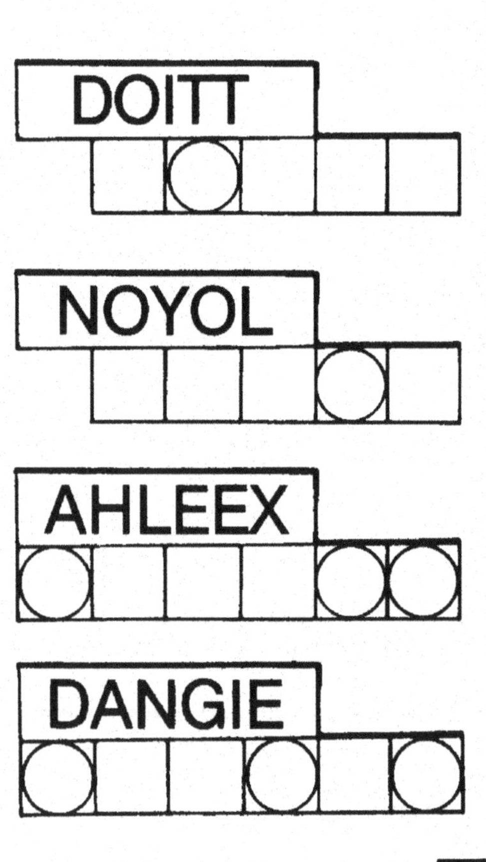
DOITT
NOYOL
AHLEEX
DANGIE

WHAT THEY WERE DOING AT THE SEWING CIRCLE.

Now arrange the circled letters to form the surprise answer, as suggested by the above cartoon.

Print answer here

PUZZLE
81

JUMBLE®

Unscramble these four Jumbles, one letter to each square, to form four ordinary words.

TYHEM
TAIRO
TRAEAK
ARUBUE
Let's take a break and go back down after lunch.
I'll be ready to dive after a bit.
AFTER SCUBA DIVING FOR HOURS, THEY WERE READY TO ---

Now arrange the circled letters to form the surprise answer, as suggested by the above cartoon.

Print answer here

PUZZLE
82

JUMBLE®

Unscramble these four Jumbles, one letter to each square, to form four ordinary words.

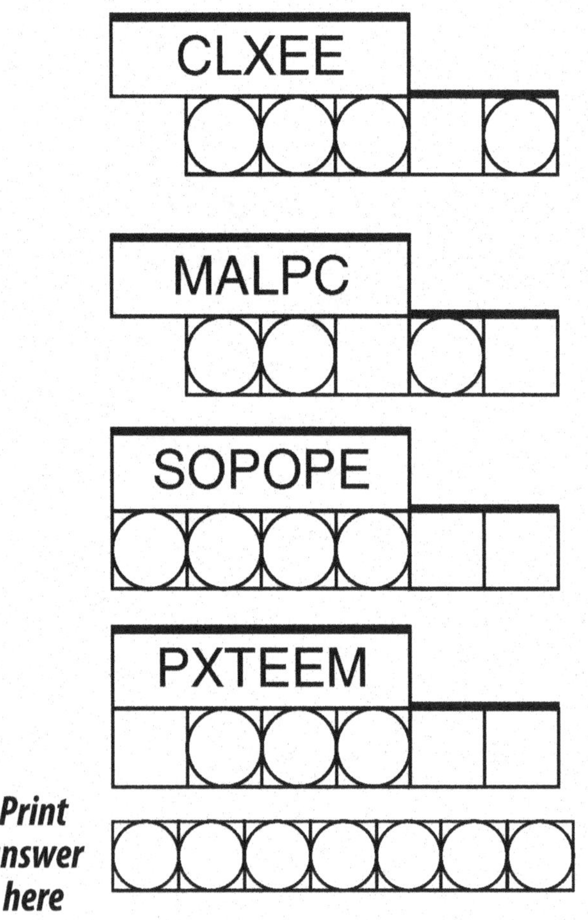
CLXEE
MALPC
SOPOPE
PXTEEM

We've named our apartments with triganomic terms. Here are the Sine and Cosine buildings.
I don't get it.
THE NEW APARTMENT BUILDINGS WERE VERY CONFUSING. IT WAS A ---

Now arrange the circled letters to form the surprise answer, as suggested by the above cartoon.

Print answer here

PUZZLE
83

JUMBLE®

Unscramble these four Jumbles, one letter to each square, to form four ordinary words.

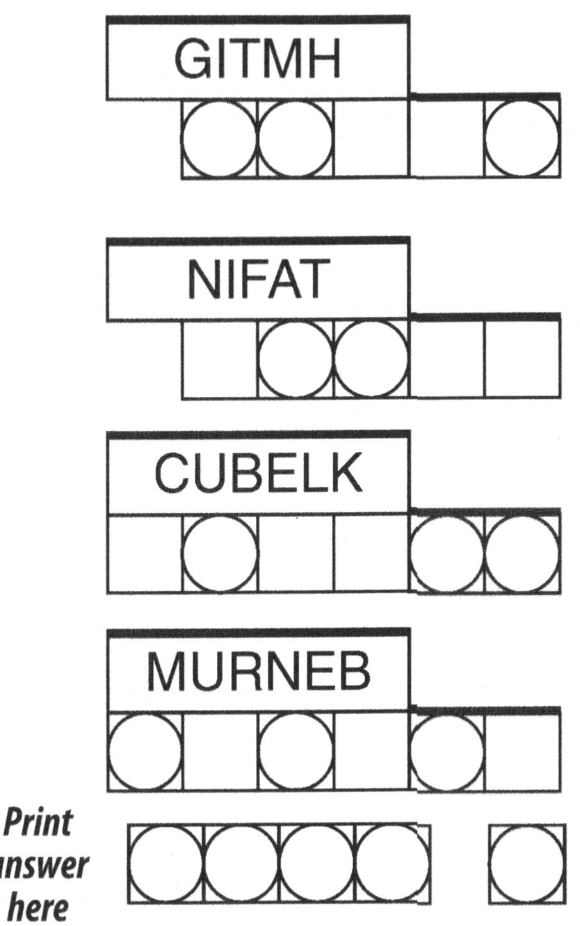

GITMH
NIFAT
CUBELK
MURNEB

You like coffee, too? What're the odds! Sometimes I like water more. But what is coffee? Hot water!
I need to drive faster so we can get to work.
THEY DROVE AT 60 MPH, AND HIS ANNOYING PASSENGER WAS TALKING A ---

Now arrange the circled letters to form the surprise answer, as suggested by the above cartoon.

Print answer here

PUZZLE
84

JUMBLE®

Unscramble these four Jumbles, one letter to each square, to form four ordinary words.

AREOP
CEFTA
CUGORH
LIMYTE
I'm done. I keep losing roommates. I'm getting a bad feeling about this place.
I've got a plan. We're busting out tonight.
THE CHICKENS WERE TIRED OF LIFE ON THE FARM AND WANTED TO ---
Print answer here

Now arrange the circled letters to form the surprise answer, as suggested by the above cartoon.

PUZZLE
85

JUMBLE®

Unscramble these four Jumbles, one letter to each square, to form four ordinary words.

NALKP
AKWEA
SHOTOE
DUTBEG
Hey, cousin! Long time no see!
Hey there!
WHEN THE OX-LIKE ANTELOPE MET UP WITH HIS FRIENDS, HE SAID ---
' " " ?

Now arrange the circled letters to form the surprise answer, as suggested by the above cartoon.

PUZZLE
86

JUMBLE®

Unscramble these four Jumbles, one letter to each square, to form four ordinary words.

TCEOT
LIHYL
CLIPEK
SKYCIT
What are these called? My kids are devouring them.
I'm thinking "Lollipop." If you don't chew them, they'll last longer.
IN 1908, GEORGE SMITH, CLAIMING HE INVENTED THE MODERN-STYLE LOLLIPOP, SOLD THEM ---

Now arrange the circled letters to form the surprise answer, as suggested by the above cartoon.

Print answer here ○○○○○○○ - ○○○○○

PUZZLE
87

JUMBLE®
OGAME
HTOOP
GNININ
CURPES
Good luck with that piece of junk.
At least I have turbo boost.
THE DESIGNERS OF THE SINGLE-PERSON BLIMPS WERE EXPERIENCING ---
Print answer here

Unscramble these four Jumbles, one letter to each square, to form four ordinary words.

Now arrange the circled letters to form the surprise answer, as suggested by the above cartoon.

PUZZLE
88

JUMBLE®

Unscramble these four Jumbles, one letter to each square, to form four ordinary words.

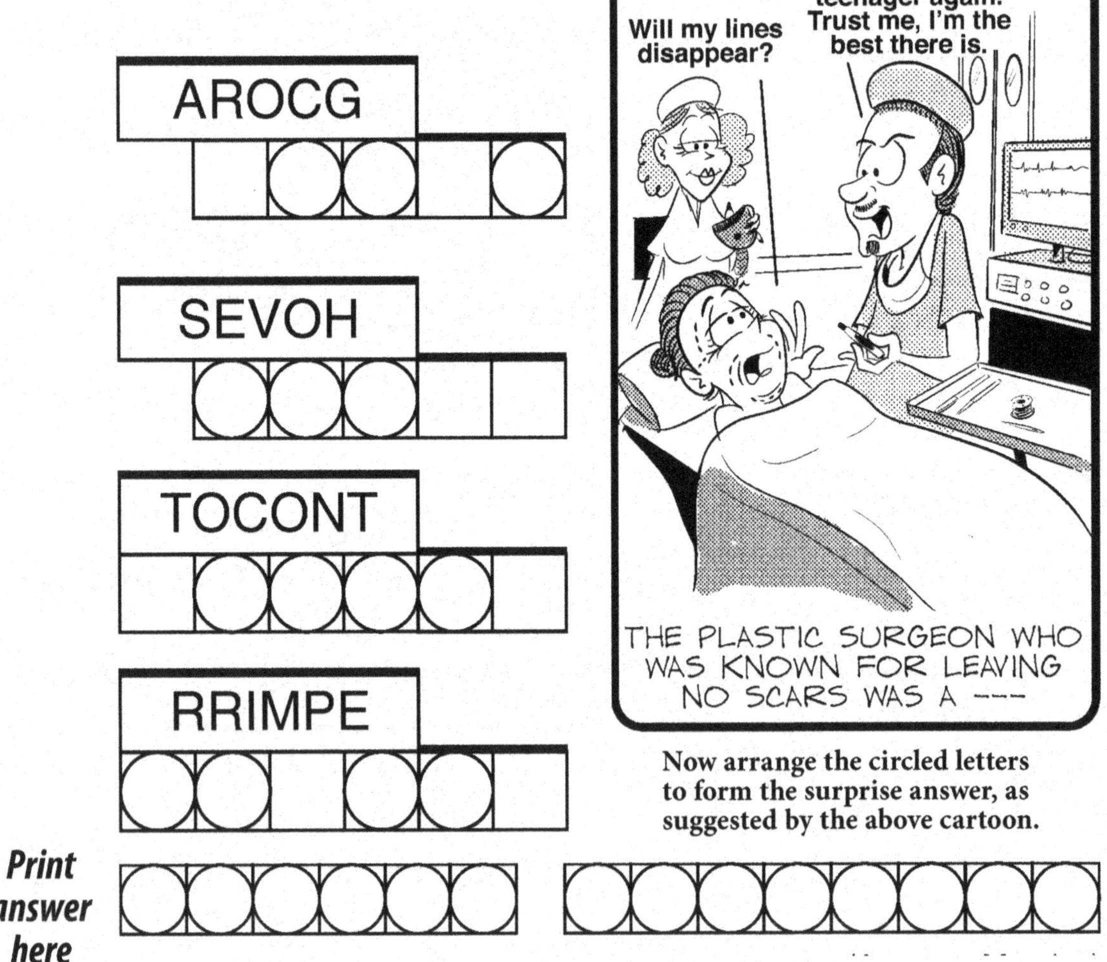
ARОCG
SEVOH
TOCONT
RRIMPE
Will my lines disappear?
You'll look like a teenager again. Trust me, I'm the best there is.
THE PLASTIC SURGEON WHO WAS KNOWN FOR LEAVING NO SCARS WAS A ---

Now arrange the circled letters to form the surprise answer, as suggested by the above cartoon.

Print answer here

PUZZLE
89

JUMBLE®

Unscramble these four Jumbles, one letter to each square, to form four ordinary words.

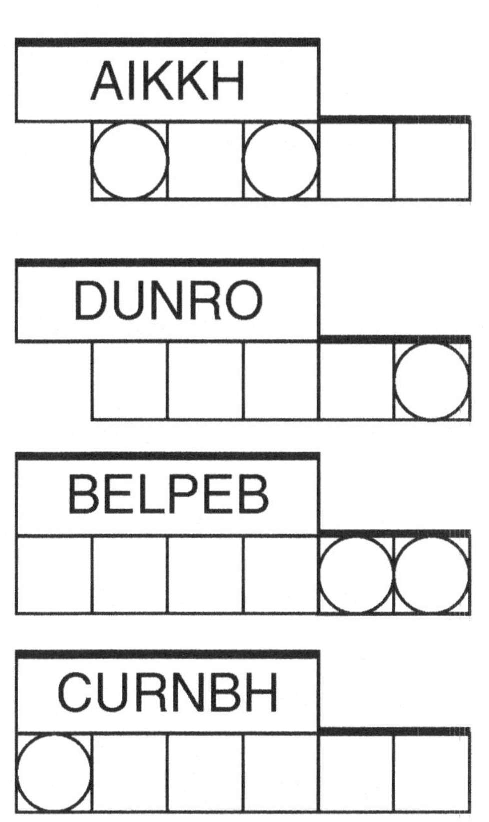
AIKKH
DUNRO
BELPEB
CURNBH

No. I think I need more now.
What? We agreed on this amount. You can't change your mind.
WHEN THE ALL-STAR PITCHER WAS PRESENTED WITH A NEW CONTRACT, HE ----

Now arrange the circled letters to form the surprise answer, as suggested by the above cartoon.

Print answer here

PUZZLE
90

JUMBLE®

Unscramble these four Jumbles, one letter to each square, to form four ordinary words.

AONPI

ZOKAO

HELMUB

DRANTS

I have a lot to choose from. Do you see anything you like?
That one right there!
SHE WAS SHOPPING FOR JUST THE RIGHT KNIFE AND WAS KEEPING A ---

Now arrange the circled letters to form the surprise answer, as suggested by the above cartoon.

Print answer here

PUZZLE
91

JUMBLE®

Unscramble these four Jumbles, one letter to each square, to form four ordinary words.

DEEWG
LUYBK
DEELYI
NNCOAY

You sound great.
A little less crowded than you're used to.
Very relaxing.
THE PIANIST PLAYED FOR JUST A FEW PEOPLE. HIS PERFORMANCE WAS ---

Now arrange the circled letters to form the surprise answer, as suggested by the above cartoon.

Print answer here 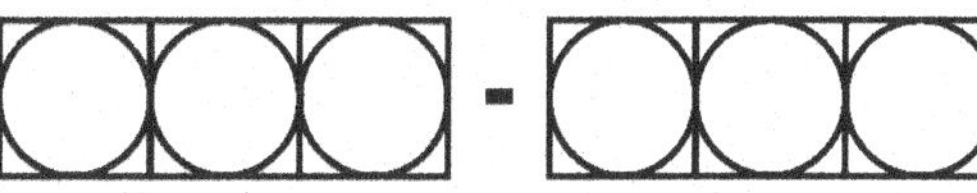

PUZZLE
92

JUMBLE®

Unscramble these four Jumbles, one letter to each square, to form four ordinary words.

POSLI

CHLSA

COYDEM

ENKIOV

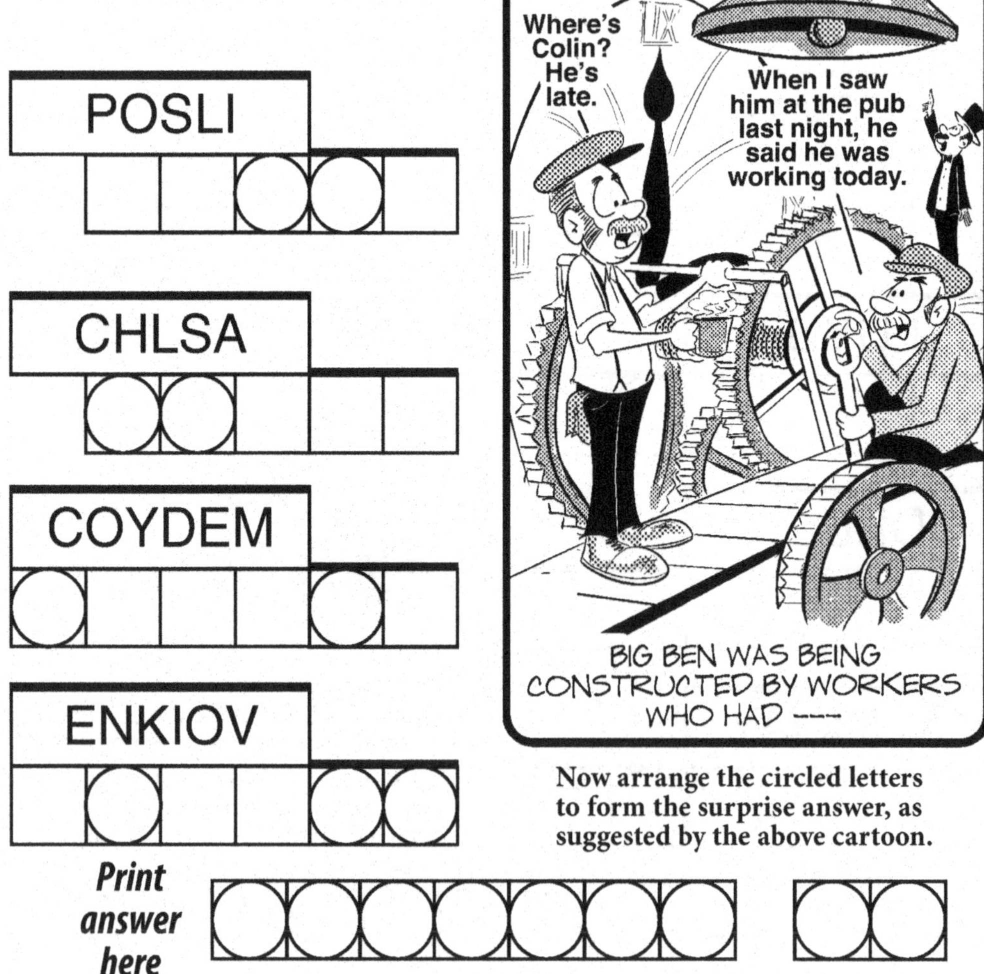
Where's Colin? He's late.
When I saw him at the pub last night, he said he was working today.
BIG BEN WAS BEING CONSTRUCTED BY WORKERS WHO HAD ---

Now arrange the circled letters to form the surprise answer, as suggested by the above cartoon.

Print answer here

PUZZLE
93

JUMBLE®

Unscramble these four Jumbles, one letter to each square, to form four ordinary words.

FNUIT

SSEEN

SONUCI

EINIDO

So, we're roomates. I'm warning you, I snore. How long are you in for?
I'm here for 20 years. I like my space. I also like to read.
THE CONVERSATION BETWEEN THE PRISON INMATES WAS MADE POSSIBLE BECAUSE OF ---

Now arrange the circled letters to form the surprise answer, as suggested by the above cartoon.

Print answer here

PUZZLE
94

JUMBLE®

Unscramble these four Jumbles, one letter to each square, to form four ordinary words.

SLEPL

POMOH

HYTMRH

ULIXFN

Are you working on your grand slam jog?
Just a little workout before heading to the park.
THE BASEBALL PLAYER LOVED HIS TREADMILL AND ALL THE ---

Now arrange the circled letters to form the surprise answer, as suggested by the above cartoon.

Print answer here

PUZZLE
95

JUMBLE®

Unscramble these four Jumbles, one letter to each square, to form four ordinary words.

YAKKA
BCELA
CENTEM
GGGYRO

Let me introduce our new CEO, Sir Topham Hatt
I've got big plans to increase our ridership.
THE RAILROAD HIRED A NEW CEO TO HELP GET ITS BUSINESS ---

Now arrange the circled letters to form the surprise answer, as suggested by the above cartoon.

Print answer here

PUZZLE
96

JUMBLE®

Unscramble these four Jumbles, one letter to each square, to form four ordinary words.

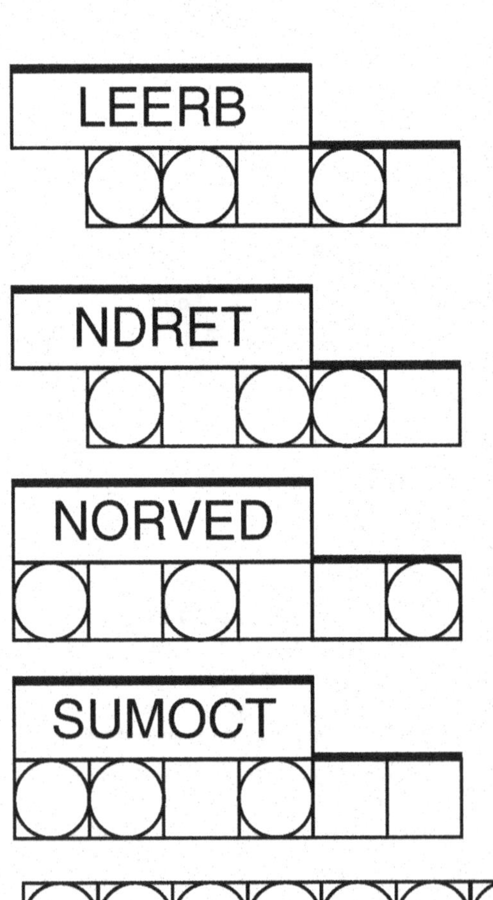
LEERB
NDRET
NORVED
SUMOCT

I wonder what they're doing back at work right now.
I think it's lunchtime.
THE FACT THAT THEY WERE TUBING DOWN THE RIVER NOW MADE IT A ---

Now arrange the circled letters to form the surprise answer, as suggested by the above cartoon.

Print answer here

PUZZLE
97

JUMBLE®

Unscramble these four Jumbles, one letter to each square, to form four ordinary words.

TUGRN

ABSIS

CFEETF

NDAYIT

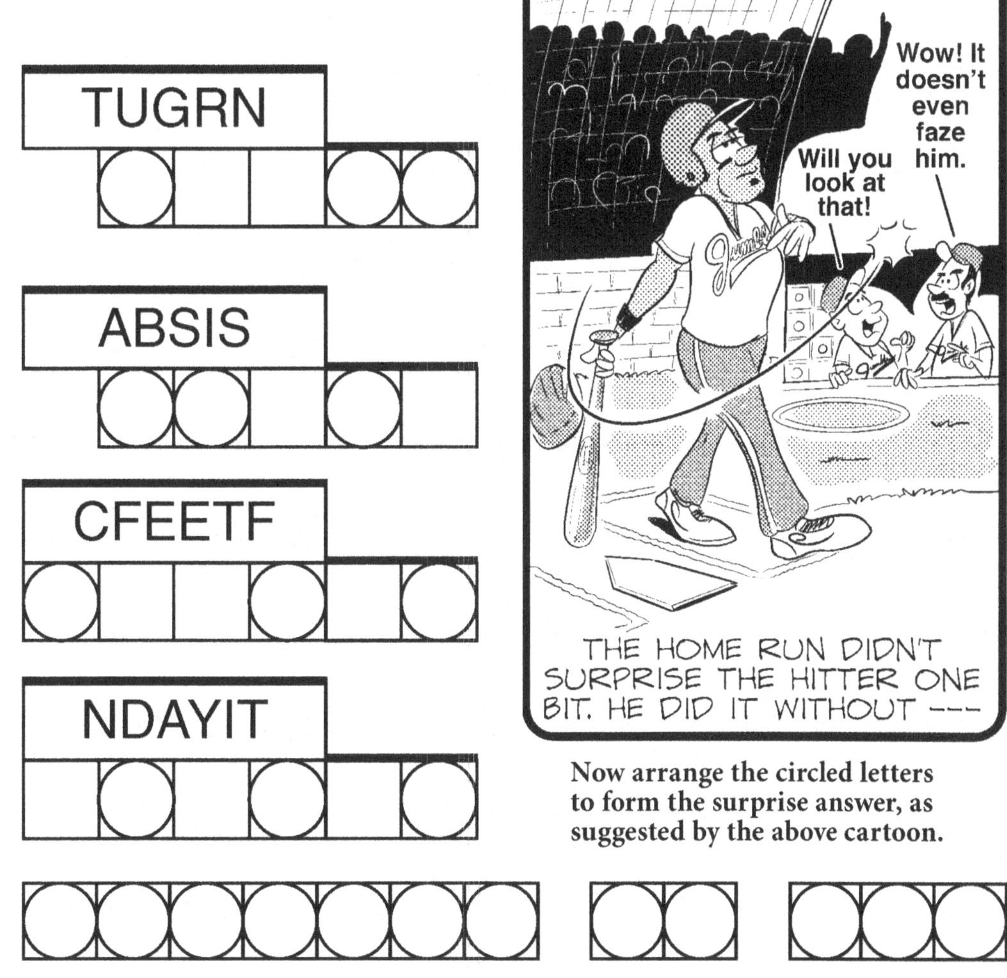
Wow! It doesn't even faze him.
Will you look at that!
THE HOME RUN DIDN'T SURPRISE THE HITTER ONE BIT. HE DID IT WITHOUT ---

Now arrange the circled letters to form the surprise answer, as suggested by the above cartoon.

Print answer here

PUZZLE
98

JUMBLE®

Unscramble these four Jumbles, one letter to each square, to form four ordinary words.

CYEDA

TEEVN

HOWSOH

LAPPOR

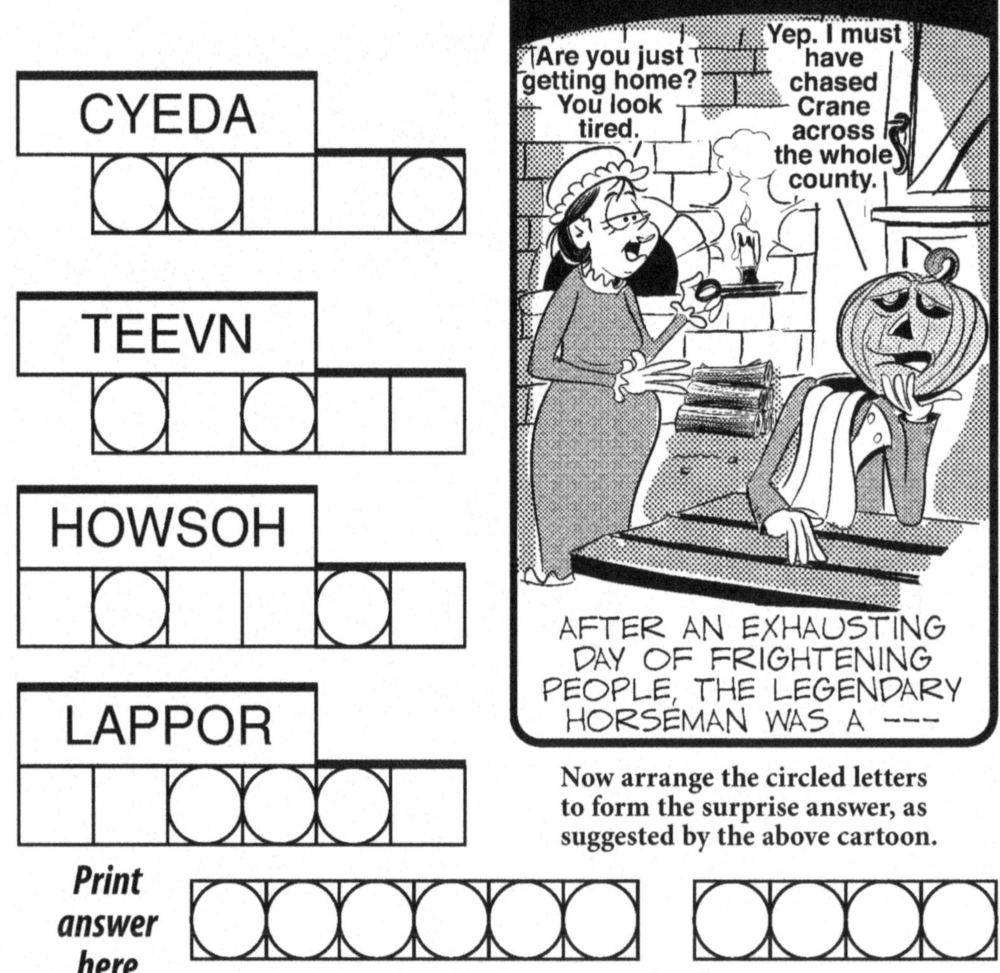
Are you just getting home? You look tired.
Yep. I must have chased Crane across the whole county.
AFTER AN EXHAUSTING DAY OF FRIGHTENING PEOPLE, THE LEGENDARY HORSEMAN WAS A ---

Now arrange the circled letters to form the surprise answer, as suggested by the above cartoon.

Print answer here

PUZZLE
99

JUMBLE®

Unscramble these four Jumbles, one letter to each square, to form four ordinary words.

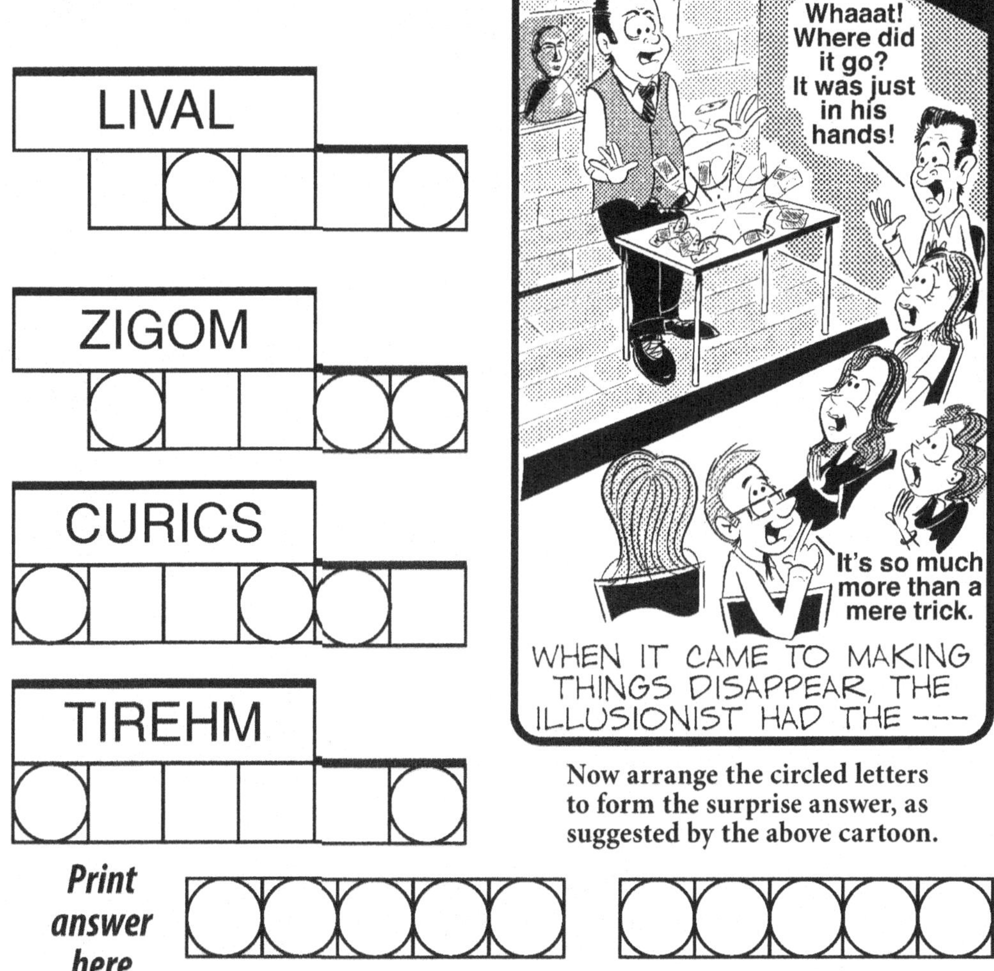
LIVAL
ZIGOM
CURICS
TIREHM
Whaaat! Where did it go? It was just in his hands!
It's so much more than a mere trick.
WHEN IT CAME TO MAKING THINGS DISAPPEAR, THE ILLUSIONIST HAD THE ---

Now arrange the circled letters to form the surprise answer, as suggested by the above cartoon.

Print answer here

PUZZLE
100

JUMBLE®

Unscramble these four Jumbles, one letter to each square, to form four ordinary words.

BEAVO
FYEHT
FRIDTA
CRIWEK
It's your choice. What do you think?
They both look great on you.
They're both so perfect.
WHEN ASKED IF SHE WANTED A RING MADE OF GOLD OR SILVER, SHE SAID ---
Now arrange the circled letters to form the surprise answer, as suggested by the above cartoon.

“ ”

PUZZLE
101

JUMBLE®

Unscramble these four Jumbles, one letter to each square, to form four ordinary words.

ASUPE
KKUSN
TOTOTA
LAPOWL
We can just go this way. He's on a stroll.
What are we going to do?
THEY WERE ABLE TO GET AWAY FROM THE PORCUPINE BECAUSE THE PORCUPINE WAS A ---

Now arrange the circled letters to form the surprise answer, as suggested by the above cartoon.

Print answer here

PUZZLE
102

JUMBLE®

Unscramble these four Jumbles, one letter to each square, to form four ordinary words.

TPEHD

DELWL

AAAPPY

FPICYA

I'm heading over to the Red Lion pub at 5 p.m.
I'll join you for sure. Looking forward to it.
Hello! May I speak with Jeff?
You've been preapproved.
THE TELEMARKETERS WOULD WORK UNTIL THEY ---

Now arrange the circled letters to form the surprise answer, as suggested by the above cartoon.

Print answer here

PUZZLE
103

JUMBLE®

Unscramble these four Jumbles, one letter to each square, to form four ordinary words.

ENZOO
LUFFF
NRRUNE
WORNDA
How about a heads up!
At least we're all together.
Join us!
WHEN EACH OF THEM HIT ONTO THE NEXT FAIRWAY, THE GOLFERS WERE ---

Now arrange the circled letters to form the surprise answer, as suggested by the above cartoon.

Print answer here “ ”

PUZZLE
104

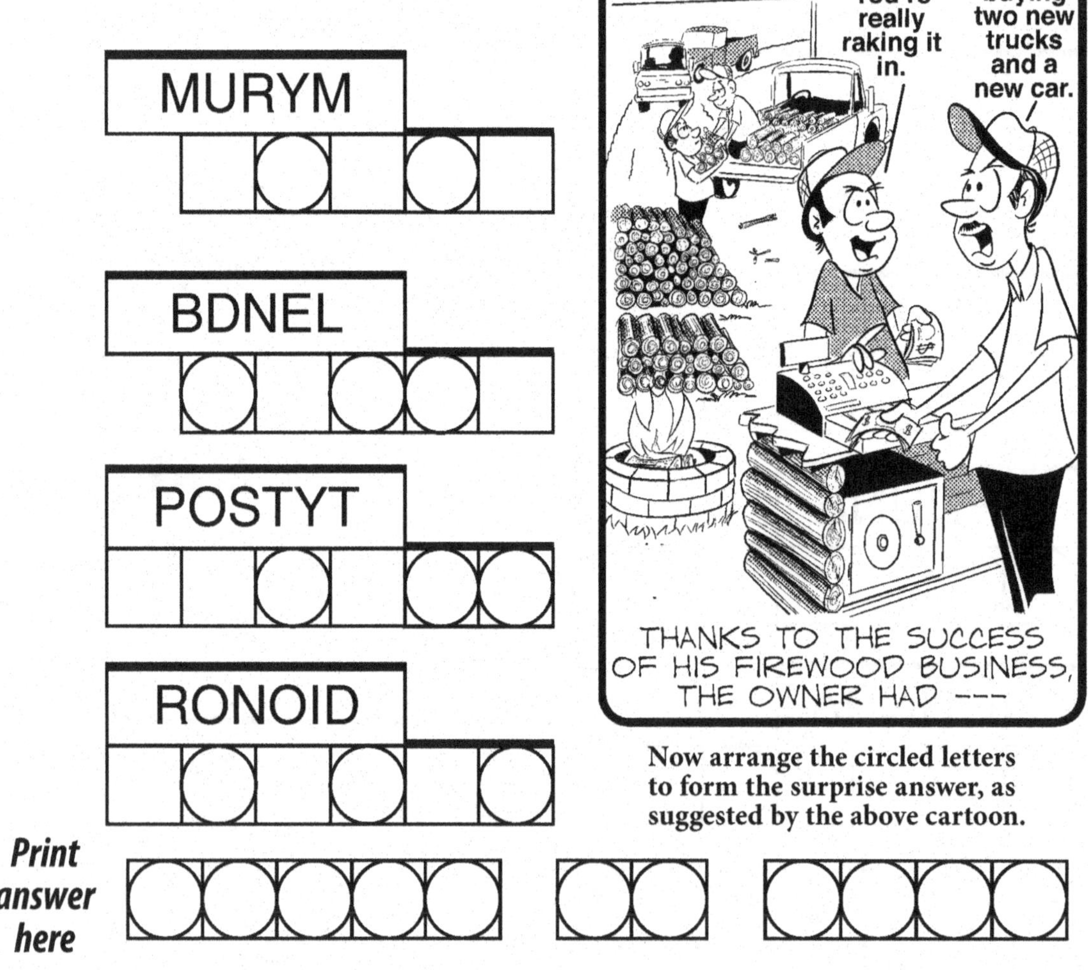
JUMBLE®
Unscramble these four Jumbles, one letter to each square, to form four ordinary words.
MURYM
BDNEL
POSTYT
RONOID
HATCHET FIREWOOD
Wow! You're really raking it in.
I'm buying two new trucks and a new car.
THANKS TO THE SUCCESS OF HIS FIREWOOD BUSINESS, THE OWNER HAD ---
Now arrange the circled letters to form the surprise answer, as suggested by the above cartoon.
Print answer here

PUZZLE
105

JUMBLE®

Unscramble these four Jumbles, one letter to each square, to form four ordinary words.

HATSS

POSUY

DYEEML

LIAPAM

Ahoy there!
Ahoy!
THEY SAID "HELLO" AS THEIR BOATS PASSED EACH OTHER ON THE ---

Now arrange the circled letters to form the surprise answer, as suggested by the above cartoon.

Print answer here " "

PUZZLE
106

JUMBLE®

Unscramble these four Jumbles, one letter to each square, to form four ordinary words.

TLATO
PHEDT
RULYXU
GRANJO
I may be a while.
What? No coffee!
Do we have any coffee yet?
It's not working!
AFTER THEIR COFFEE GRINDER BROKE, BUSINESS AT THE COFFEE SHOP ---

Now arrange the circled letters to form the surprise answer, as suggested by the above cartoon.

Print answer here

PUZZLE
107

JUMBLE®

Unscramble these four Jumbles, one letter to each square, to form four ordinary words.

HISSW
SERSD
WHERSD
BETOCJ
Where's the coil?
I thought you said you were bringing it!
THE CONFUSION BETWEEN THE ELECTRICIANS WAS A RESULT OF THEM GETTING THEIR ---

Now arrange the circled letters to form the surprise answer, as suggested by the above cartoon.

Print answer here

PUZZLE
108

JUMBLE®

Unscramble these four Jumbles, one letter to each square, to form four ordinary words.

GEZAL
WATIA
PNDORA
DUIEMM

I love the color! Very realistic.
It's my special blend.
TO CREATE THE PAINTING OF THE HOG, THE ARTIST NEEDED JUST THE RIGHT ---

Now arrange the circled letters to form the surprise answer, as suggested by the above cartoon.

Print answer here 

PUZZLE
109

JUMBLE®

Unscramble these four Jumbles, one letter to each square, to form four ordinary words.

KHAYS

TPRAA

CYRITK

ICEJNT

What do you think? They're our new uniform trousers!
Oh, my.
Do they make those in jeans?
TO PROMOTE HIS BUSINESS, THE LOCKSMITH WORE ---

Now arrange the circled letters to form the surprise answer, as suggested by the above cartoon.

Print answer here "◯◯◯-◯◯◯" ◯◯◯◯◯

PUZZLE
110

JUMBLE®

Unscramble these four Jumbles, one letter to each square, to form four ordinary words.

TOODU

UGBOM

WILPOL

NALETD

I thought it was too quiet in here. Put them back.
Cookies

THE TWINS GOT IN TROUBLE A LOT. THEY WERE OFTEN ---

Now arrange the circled letters to form the surprise answer, as suggested by the above cartoon.

Print answer here ◯◯ "◯◯◯" ◯◯ ◯◯◯◯

PUZZLE
111

JUMBLE®

Unscramble these four Jumbles, one letter to each square, to form four ordinary words.

GRYOL

PRUEP

SEOUDX

EYXNOG

Aren't they beautiful? This is my best crop ever.
I need to post this picture.
THE FARMER VIEWED HIS FIELD OF PUMPKINS. TO HIM, IT WAS ---

Now arrange the circled letters to form the surprise answer, as suggested by the above cartoon.

Print answer here “ ◯◯◯◯◯ - ◯◯◯◯◯ ”

PUZZLE
112

JUMBLE®

Unscrambled these four Jumbles, one letter to each square, to form four ordinary words.

BOYHB

SIHOT

GRAAUJ

NINETT

You're going down.
I want a clean fight. No hitting below the belt.
Let's go!
THE BOXING MATCH HADN'T STARTED YET, BUT IT WAS ---

Now arrange the circled letters to form the surprise answer, as suggested by the above cartoon.

Print answer here "[ ]-[ ][ ][ ][ ]" [ ][ ] [ ][ ][ ][ ][ ]

PUZZLE
113

JUMBLE
Unscramble these four Jumbles, one letter to each square, to form four ordinary words.
SYBSO
TRAYD
SACAUB
SCAWEH
Next, I have Molly, Norman, Oliver and Percy.
Wow! You did that so quickly!
He's a smart one.
FOR THE SMART CHILD, LEARNING TO PUT THINGS IN ALPHABETICAL ORDER WAS ---
Now arrange the circled letters to form the surprise answer, as suggested by the above cartoon.
Print answer here

PUZZLE
114

JUMBLE®

Unscramble these four Jumbles, one letter to each square, to form four ordinary words.

AANCL
OGYEO
GSORNT
CIHWST
How'd you write a tale more than 1,100 pages?
How much time do you have?
WHEN ASKED WHAT INSPIRED HIM TO WRITE A LENGTHY BOOK, J.R.R. TOLKIEN SAID ---

Now arrange the circled letters to form the surprise answer, as suggested by the above cartoon.

Print answer here

PUZZLE
115

JUMBLE®

Unscramble these four Jumbles, one letter to each square, to form four ordinary words.

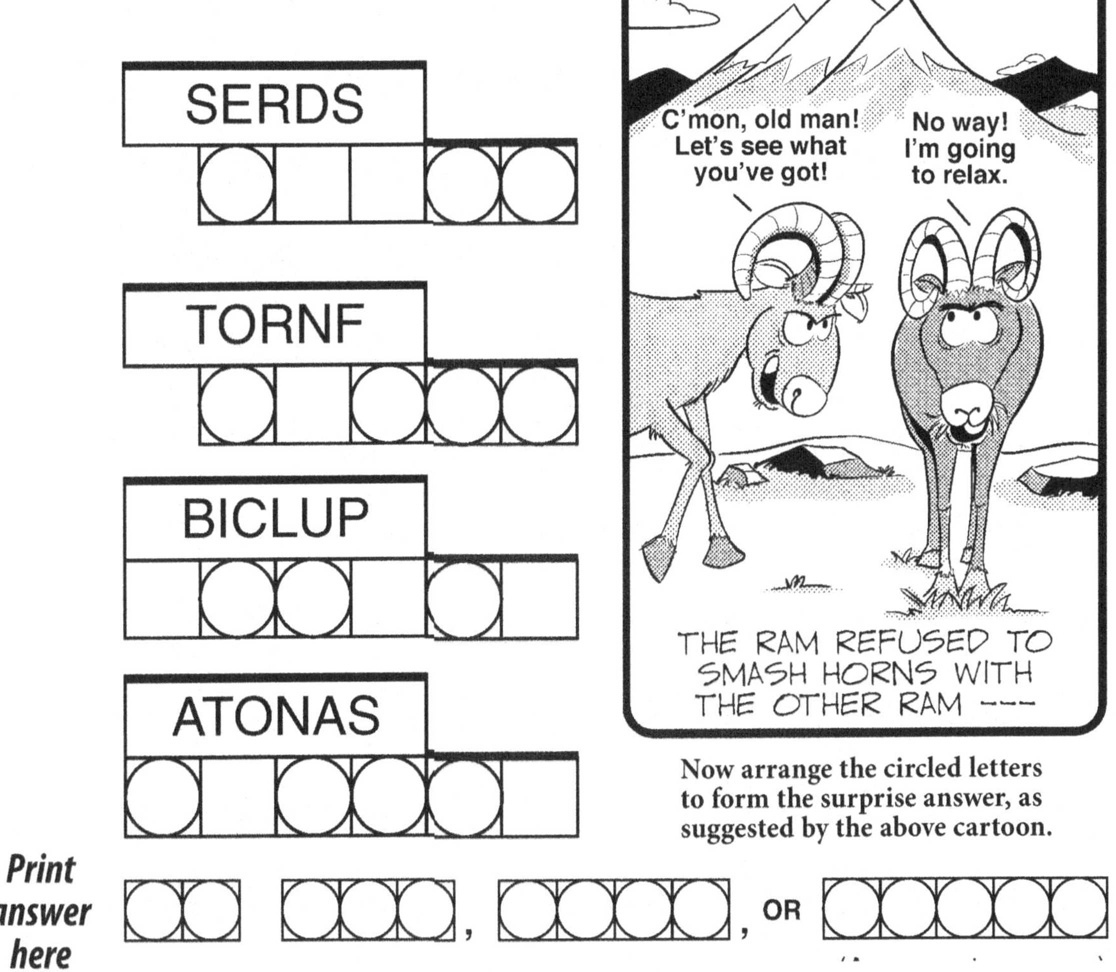
SERDS
TORNF
BICLUP
ATONAS
C'mon, old man! Let's see what you've got!
No way! I'm going to relax.
THE RAM REFUSED TO SMASH HORNS WITH THE OTHER RAM ---

Now arrange the circled letters to form the surprise answer, as suggested by the above cartoon.

Print answer here ○○ ○○○, ○○○○○, OR ○○○○○

PUZZLE
116

JUMBLE®

Unscramble these four Jumbles, one letter to each square, to form four ordinary words.

MATUG
ANBIC
SHARKN
CYREEL
What are you going to do about our list of demands?
We can only take care of a few of your demands.
FOR SAFETY'S SAKE, THE COAL-COMPANY OWNERS AGREED TO MAKE SOME ---

Now arrange the circled letters to form the surprise answer, as suggested by the above cartoon.

Print answer here

PUZZLE
117

JUMBLE®

Unscramble these four Jumbles, one letter to each square, to form four ordinary words.

ENPUR
DIBEA
FAYSET
TIMYUN
Hello! Our parties have an announcement to make.
Together, we've written a great bill.
Is this for real?
IF POLITICIANS WORKED TOGETHER TO SOLVE PROBLEMS, THEN THEY COULD SAY ---

Now arrange the circled letters to form the surprise answer, as suggested by the above cartoon.

Print answer here " ◯◯◯ " - ◯◯◯◯◯◯◯◯

PUZZLE
118

JUMBLE®

Unscramble these four Jumbles, one letter to each square, to form four ordinary words.

GNEBU

SUHEO

SMIRPH

VTINEN

Some examples are: ran, walked, sang, talked and learned. There are lots more. They represent action.
DREW
WRITE
TAUGHT
All right already. We get it.
THE TEACHER WAS EXPLAINING ACTION WORDS TO THE STUDENTS AND WAS BEING ---

Now arrange the circled letters to form the surprise answer, as suggested by the above cartoon.

Print answer here

PUZZLE
119

JUMBLE®

Unscramble these four Jumbles, one letter to each square, to form four ordinary words.

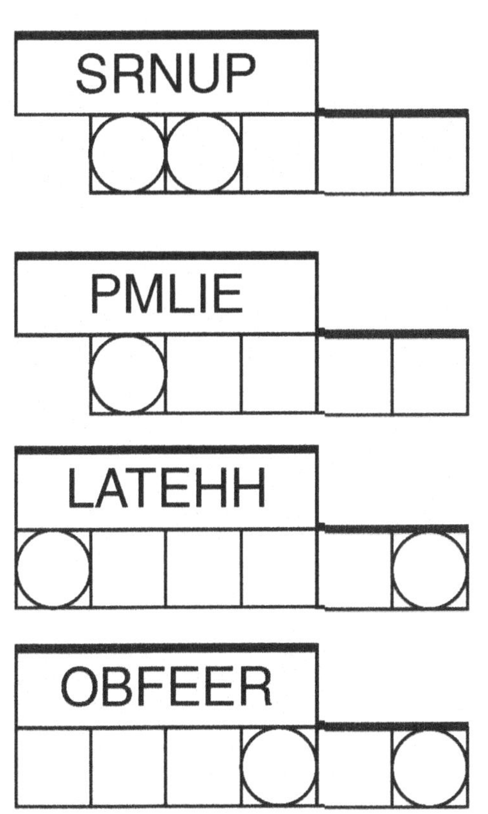
SRNUP
PMLIE
LATEHH
OBFEER

Now's your chance! Go say, "Hello!"
I'll do it!
He's looking at you, again.
HE REALLY WANTED TO SAY HELLO TO THE WOMAN AND HAD ---

Now arrange the circled letters to form the surprise answer, as suggested by the above cartoon.

Print answer here "  " 

PUZZLE
120

JUMBLE®

Unscramble these four Jumbles, one letter to each square, to form four ordinary words.

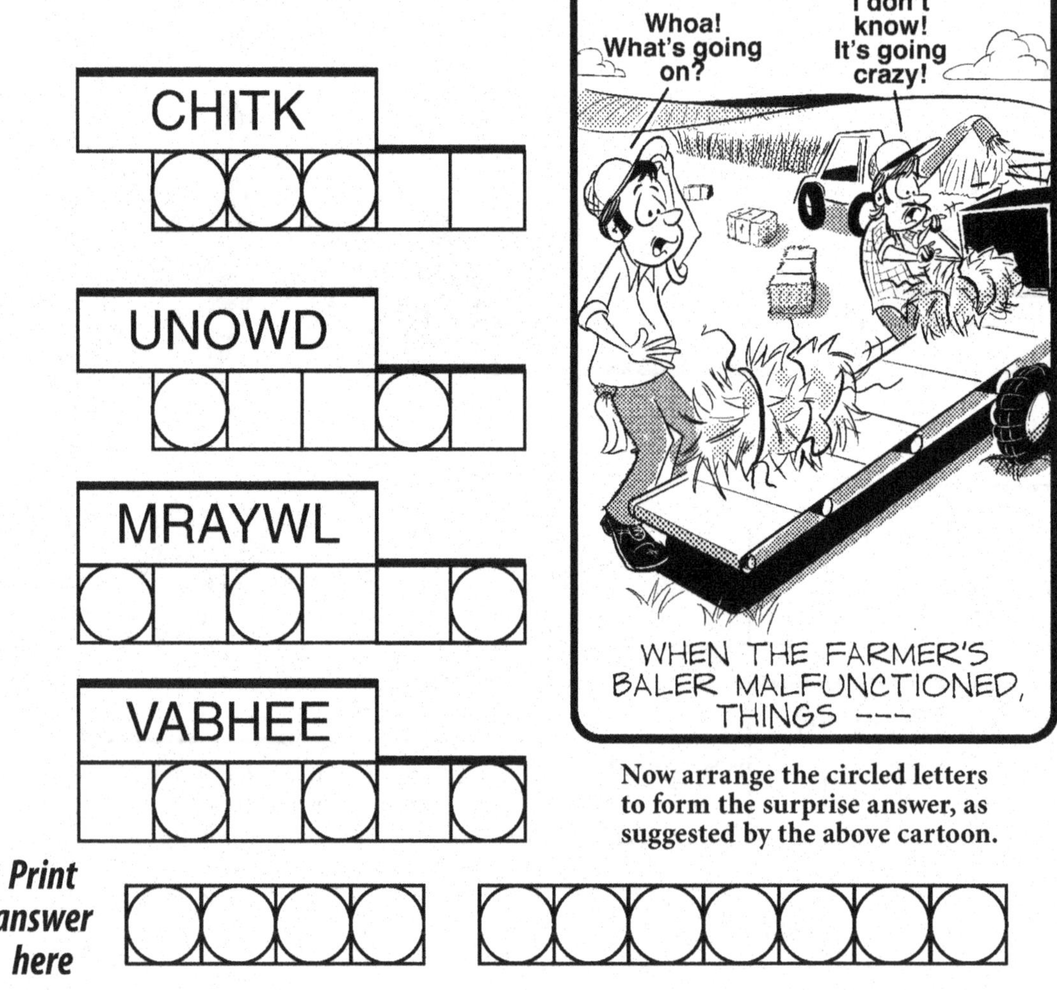
CHITK
UNOWD
MRAYWL
VABHEE
Whoa! What's going on?
I don't know! It's going crazy!
WHEN THE FARMER'S BALER MALFUNCTIONED, THINGS ---

Now arrange the circled letters to form the surprise answer, as suggested by the above cartoon.

Print answer here

PUZZLE
121

JUMBLE®

Unscramble these four Jumbles, one letter to each square, to form four ordinary words.

CARKO

TXSYI

NKREEL

HARRET

Once we get going, it will get easier.
The stones keep rolling off.
THE STONE WALL WOULD EVENTUALLY GET FINISHED, IN SPITE OF THE ---

Now arrange the circled letters to form the surprise answer, as suggested by the above cartoon.

Print answer here

PUZZLE
122

JUMBLE®

Unscramble these four Jumbles, one letter to each square, to form four ordinary words.

TIODT
SERHF
UBANDO
ENOBMA
I can't believe it holds by just squeezing it together.
It's amazing!
It replicates burrs that stick to your stockings.
WHEN VELCRO WAS INVENTED, PEOPLE WERE ---
Print answer here

Now arrange the circled letters to form the surprise answer, as suggested by the above cartoon.

PUZZLE
123

JUMBLE®

Unscramble these four Jumbles, one letter to each square, to form four ordinary words.

LHYYS

OTBUD

ALENDH

GLEHIS

This was all formed during the Ice Age.
I love the ancient ruins.
Have you ever seen the Loch Ness monster?
THE SCOTTISH HIGHLANDS' LAND FORMATIONS ARE AS ---

Now arrange the circled letters to form the surprise answer, as suggested by the above cartoon.

Print answer here ○○○ AS ○○○ ○○○○○

PUZZLE
124

JUMBLE®

Unscramble these four Jumbles, one letter to each square, to form four ordinary words.

LEEDU

YREDB

BIGRTH

YLITFH

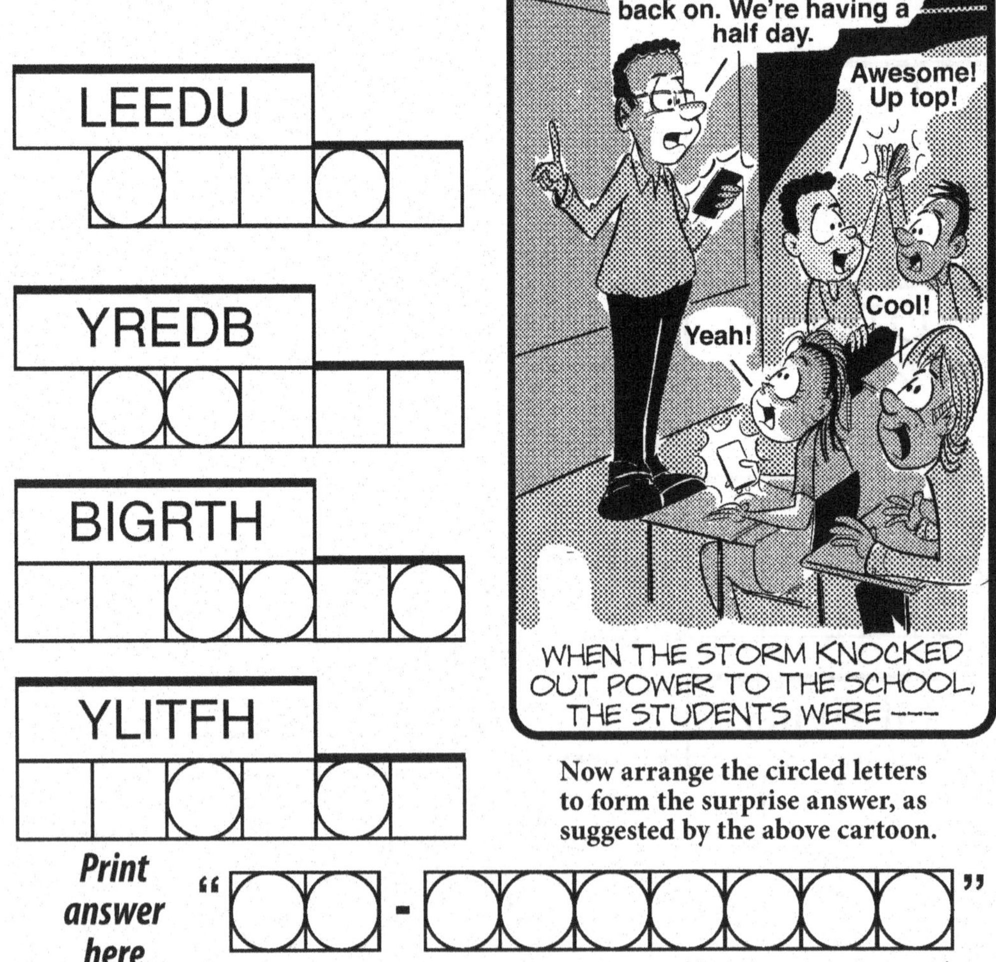
The power is not coming back on. We're having a half day.
Awesome! Up top!
Cool!
Yeah!
WHEN THE STORM KNOCKED OUT POWER TO THE SCHOOL, THE STUDENTS WERE ---

Now arrange the circled letters to form the surprise answer, as suggested by the above cartoon.

Print answer here "◯◯-◯◯◯◯◯◯◯"

PUZZLE
125

JUMBLE®

Unscramble these four Jumbles, one letter to each square, to form four ordinary words.

VONEY

USEQT

MUTUNA

EGDELP

NASHVILLE
I've been married four years now, and it's getting pretty serious.
Nate's always been there for me.
He's so nice!
THE COMEDIAN WAS WELL-RESPECTED. EVERYONE CONSIDERED HIM TO BE A---

Now arrange the circled letters to form the surprise answer, as suggested by the above cartoon.

Print answer here

PUZZLE
126

JUMBLE®

Unscramble these four Jumbles, one letter to each square, to form four ordinary words.

DARAW

RUCNH

THEKCS

LORENL

Here they are. Right where I left them.
SHE KEPT HER GLOVES BY THE DOOR SO THEY WOULD BE ---

Now arrange the circled letters to form the surprise answer, as suggested by the above cartoon.

Print answer here

PUZZLE
127

JUMBLE®

Unscramble these four Jumbles, one letter to each square, to form four ordinary words.

BAOMM

DUYDB

TARILU

SLENUS

I can't stand using these.
It makes me feel like a hamster.
THEY DIDN'T LIKE RUNNING AT THE HEALTH CLUB. TO THEM, THE MACHINE WAS A ---

Now arrange the circled letters to form the surprise answer, as suggested by the above cartoon.

Print answer here "◯◯◯◯◯-◯◯◯◯"

PUZZLE
128

JUMBLE®

Unscramble these four Jumbles, one letter to each square, to form four ordinary words.

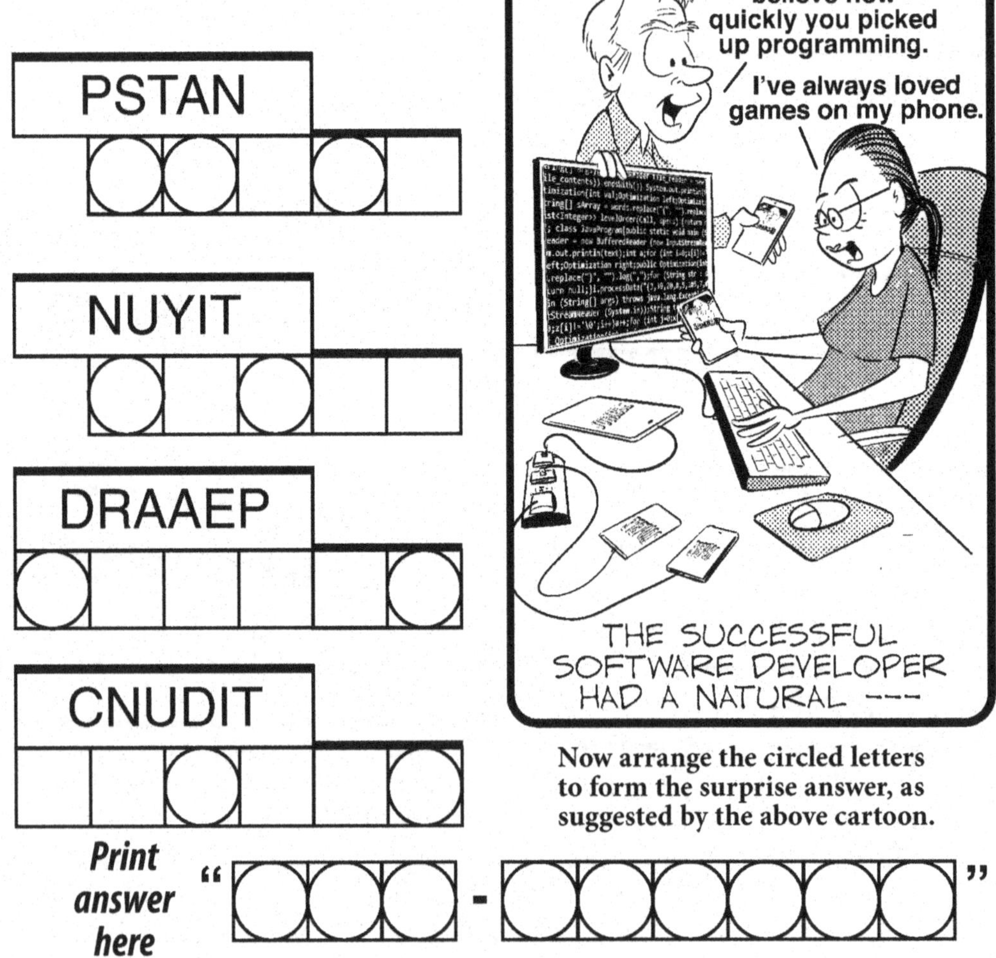
PSTAN
NUYIT
DRAAEP
CNUDIT
Wow! I can't believe how quickly you picked up programming.
I've always loved games on my phone.
THE SUCCESSFUL SOFTWARE DEVELOPER HAD A NATURAL ---

Now arrange the circled letters to form the surprise answer, as suggested by the above cartoon.

Print answer here " ◯◯◯-◯◯◯◯◯◯◯ "

PUZZLE
129

JUMBLE®
Unscramble these four Jumbles, one letter to each square, to form four ordinary words.
VPOER
SROCS
POXEES
PLAJOY
I'm so glad we're here!
What a crowd!
HE SANK THE WINNING THREE-POINT SHOT IN FRONT OF ---
Now arrange the circled letters to form the surprise answer, as suggested by the above cartoon.
Print answer here
OF

PUZZLE
130

JUMBLE®

Unscramble these four Jumbles, one letter to each square, to form four ordinary words.

NYALM

DIYLO

TFROGE

TRATEO

Poppy and Lee Lee love our tradition of decorating the tree together.
This is so much fun!
Can I have one?
THEY SPENT THE DAY WITH THEIR DAUGHTER'S CHILDREN AND HAD A ---

Now arrange the circled letters to form the surprise answer, as suggested by the above cartoon.

Print answer here

PUZZLE
131

JUMBLE®

Unscramble these four Jumbles, one letter to each square, to form four ordinary words.

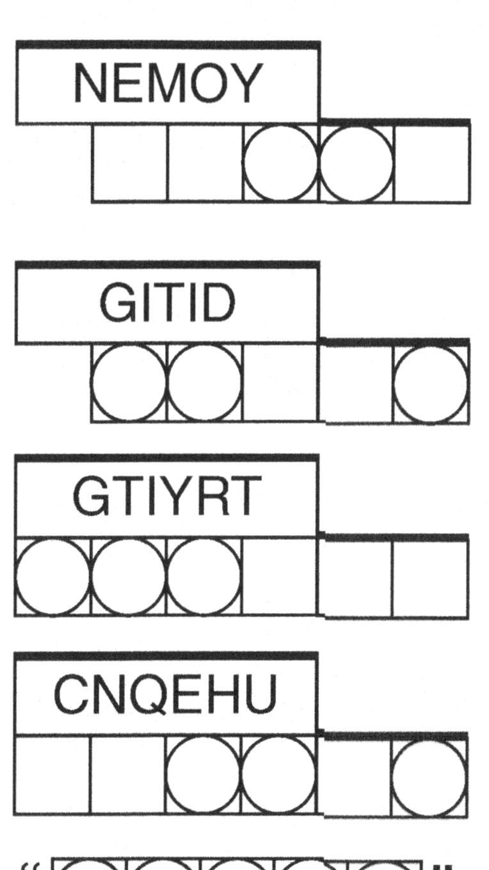
NEMOY
GITID
GTIYRT
CNQEHU

I love sushi!
WITH EACH TENTACLE HOLDING FOOD, THE OCTOPUS ---

Now arrange the circled letters to form the surprise answer, as suggested by the above cartoon.

Print answer here  HIS

PUZZLE
132

JUMBLE®

Unscramble these four Jumbles, one letter to each square, to form four ordinary words.

YAOLR

UHNBC

NASOSE

SLUDOH

I need to catch a largemouth now. It's almost time to go to the concert.
I'm stuck in the reeds again.
THE WOODWIND PLAYER WENT FISHING WITH HIS BUDDY AND HOPED TO CATCH A ---

Now arrange the circled letters to form the surprise answer, as suggested by the above cartoon.

Print answer here

PUZZLE
133

JUMBLE®

Unscramble these four Jumbles, one letter to each square, to form four ordinary words.

PRUNS

SATEE

LNAFEL

YUSANE

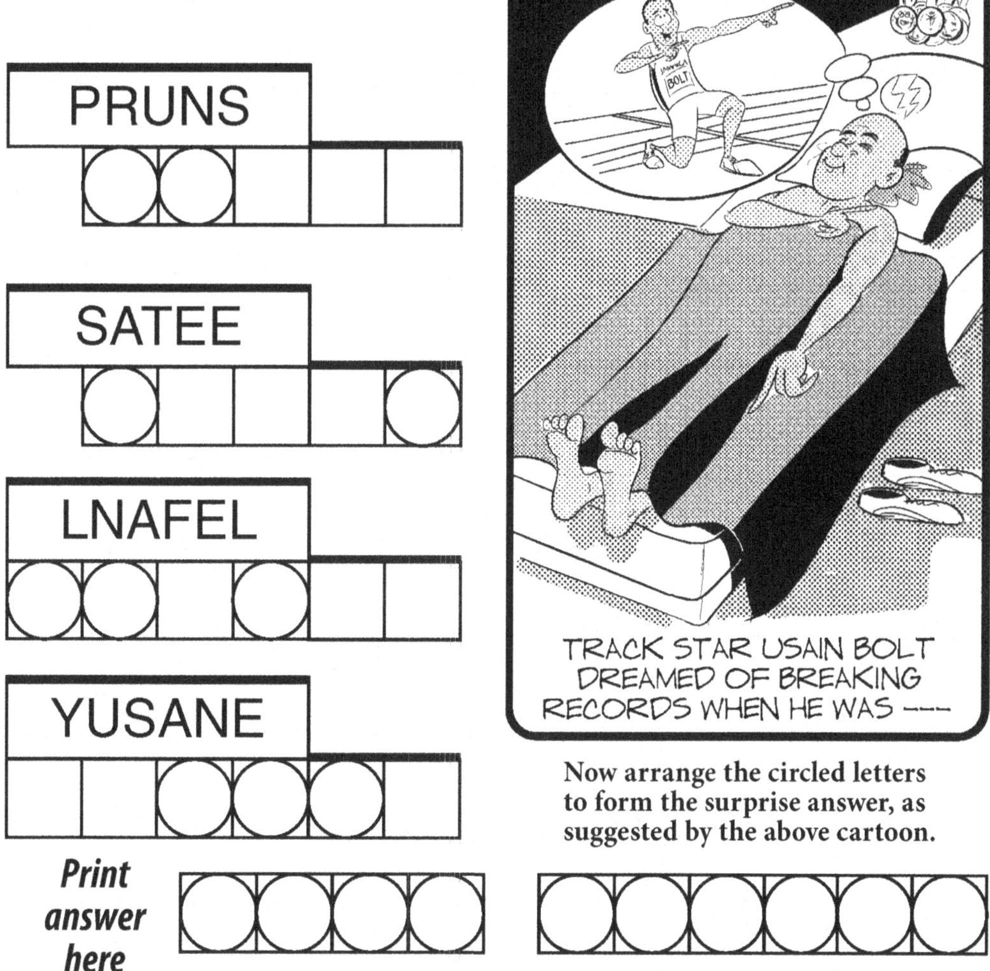
BOLT
TRACK STAR USAIN BOLT DREAMED OF BREAKING RECORDS WHEN HE WAS ---

Now arrange the circled letters to form the surprise answer, as suggested by the above cartoon.

Print answer here

PUZZLE
134

JUMBLE®

Unscramble these four Jumbles, one letter to each square, to form four ordinary words.

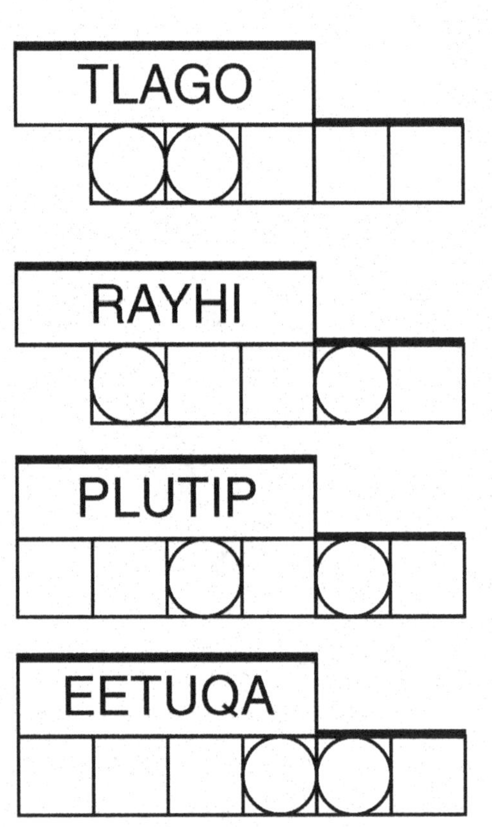

TLAGO
RAYHI
PLUTIP
EETUQA

So, how did you do on your math test?
OK, I guess, if 100% is pretty good.
Wow!
100% A+
I ♥ JUMBLE
AFTER ACING THE MATH TEST, HER PARENTS ASKED HOW SHE DID, AND SHE ANSWERED ---

Now arrange the circled letters to form the surprise answer, as suggested by the above cartoon.

Print answer here

PUZZLE
135

JUMBLE®

Unscramble these four Jumbles, one letter to each square, to form four ordinary words.

USIES

MIYDL

LHIRTL

BLAYBF

XXX
THE PAINTING OF THE MOONSHINER'S EQUIPMENT WAS A ---

Now arrange the circled letters to form the surprise answer, as suggested by the above cartoon.

Print answer here

PUZZLE
136

JUMBLE®

Unscramble these four Jumbles, one letter to each square, to form four ordinary words.

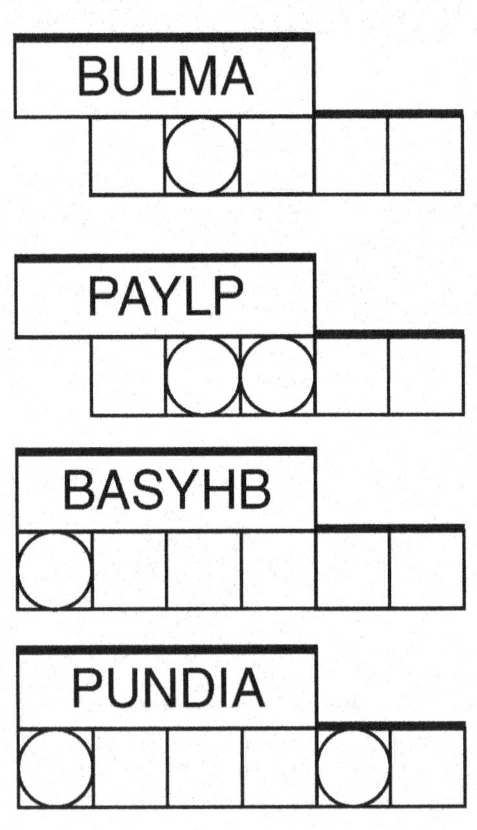
BULMA
PAYLP
BASYHB
PUNDIA

Light rays entering the eye are absorbed by the tissues directly inside the eye.
Is this going to be on the test?
THE FUTURE EYE DOCTORS WERE ---

Now arrange the circled letters to form the surprise answer, as suggested by the above cartoon.

Print answer here

PUZZLE
137

JUMBLE®

Unscramble these four Jumbles, one letter to each square, to form four ordinary words.

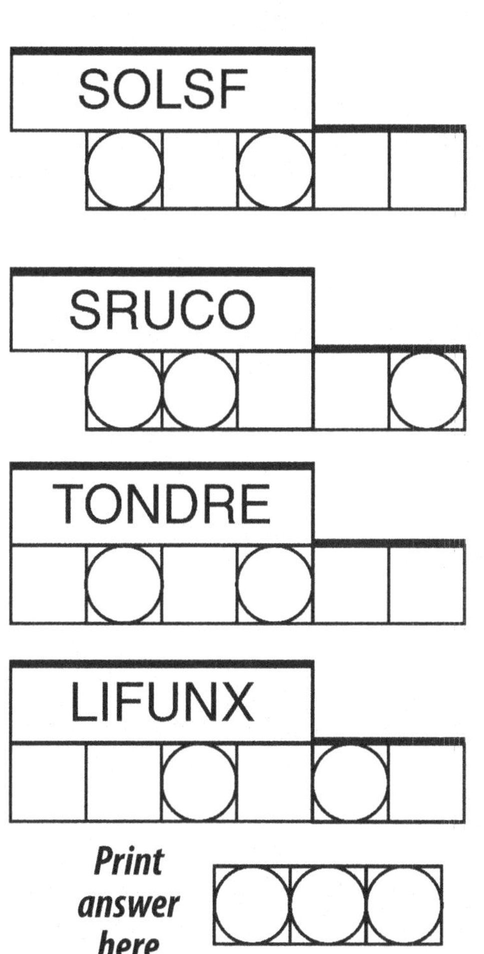
SOLSF
SRUCO
TONDRE
LIFUNX

Dolly, I don't think you're supposed to hit it out of a backyard.
I've got this, Matt.
THE GOLFER'S TEE SHOT ENDED UP IN A YARD AS A RESULT OF IT BEING HIT ---

Now arrange the circled letters to form the surprise answer, as suggested by the above cartoon.

Print answer here

PUZZLE
138

JUMBLE®

Unscramble these four Jumbles, one letter to each square, to form four ordinary words.

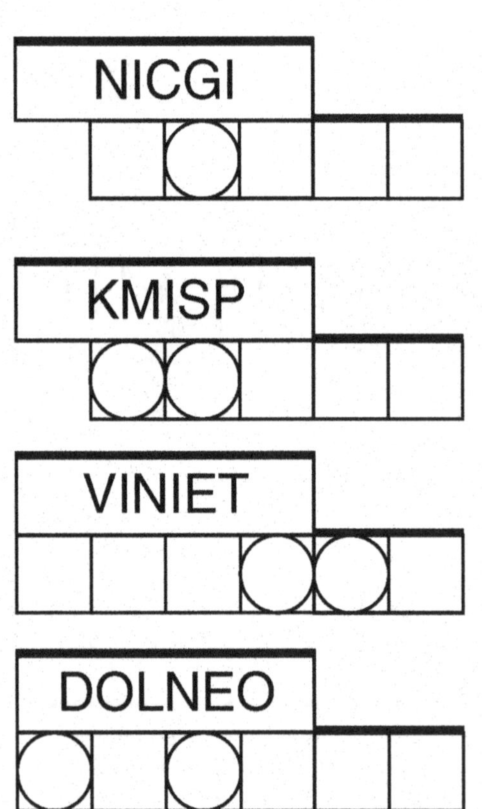
NICGI
KMISP
VINIET
DOLNEO

JUM +15
SDKO -20
XWRDS -8
WRDSRCH -13.5
I need 2,000 shares of IBM. Can you do that?
I've got plenty.
YOU CAN BUY SHARES OF IBM BECAUSE THE EXCHANGE HAS PLENTY --

Now arrange the circled letters to form the surprise answer, as suggested by the above cartoon.

Print answer here  

PUZZLE
139

JUMBLE®

Unscramble these four Jumbles, one letter to each square, to form four ordinary words.

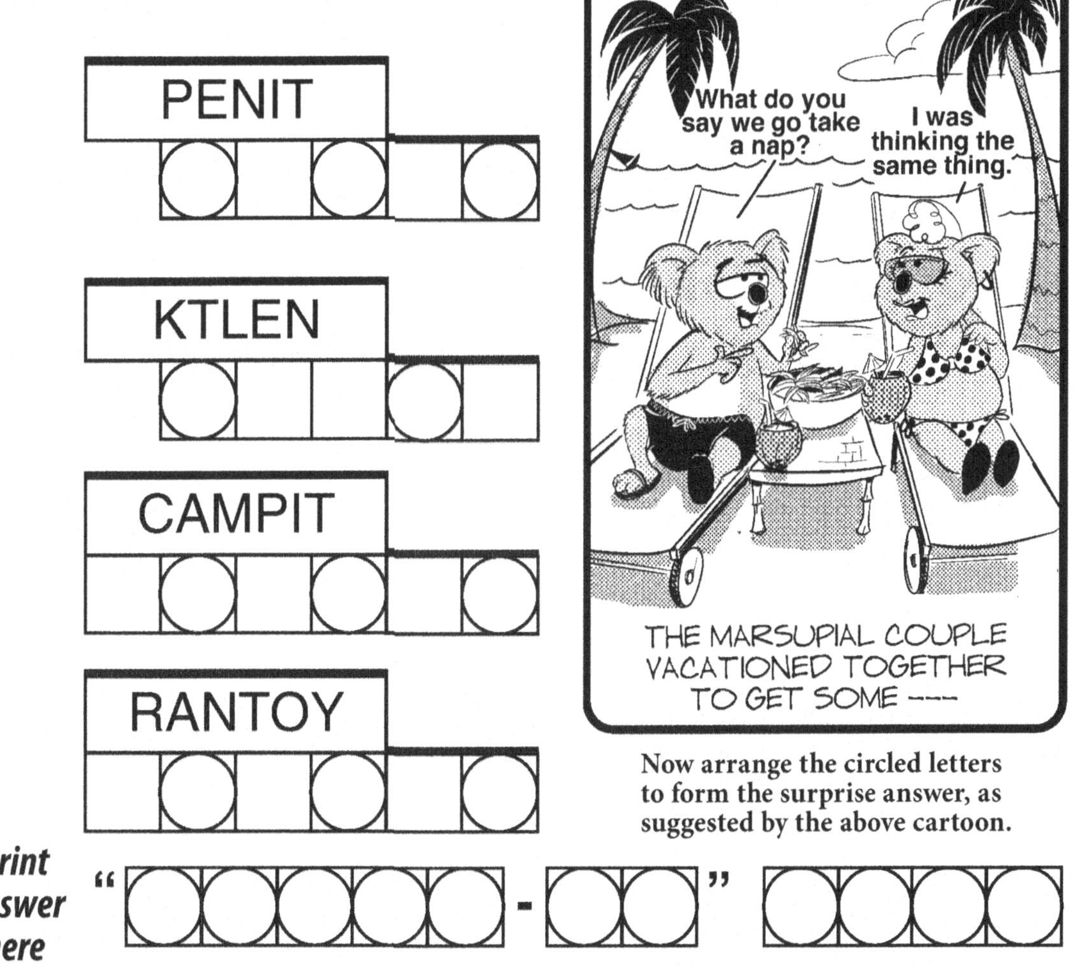
PENIT
KTLEN
CAMPIT
RANTOY
What do you say we go take a nap?
I was thinking the same thing.
THE MARSUPIAL COUPLE VACATIONED TOGETHER TO GET SOME ---
Print answer here

Now arrange the circled letters to form the surprise answer, as suggested by the above cartoon.

PUZZLE
140

JUMBLE®

Unscramble these four Jumbles, one letter to each square, to form four ordinary words.

NANLU

BKALE

AGAMDE

CYWRES

He eats a chrysalis and has a butterfly in his stomach.
I know exactly what to do.
WILCO
THERE'S A JUMBLE CARTOON EACH DAY BECAUSE THE ARTIST HAS NEVER ---

Now arrange the circled letters to form the surprise answer, as suggested by the above cartoon.

Print answer here

PUZZLE
141

JUMBLE®

Unscramble these four Jumbles, one letter to each square, to form four ordinary words.

CIWEN

SIRKB

CTANAV

PEDANX

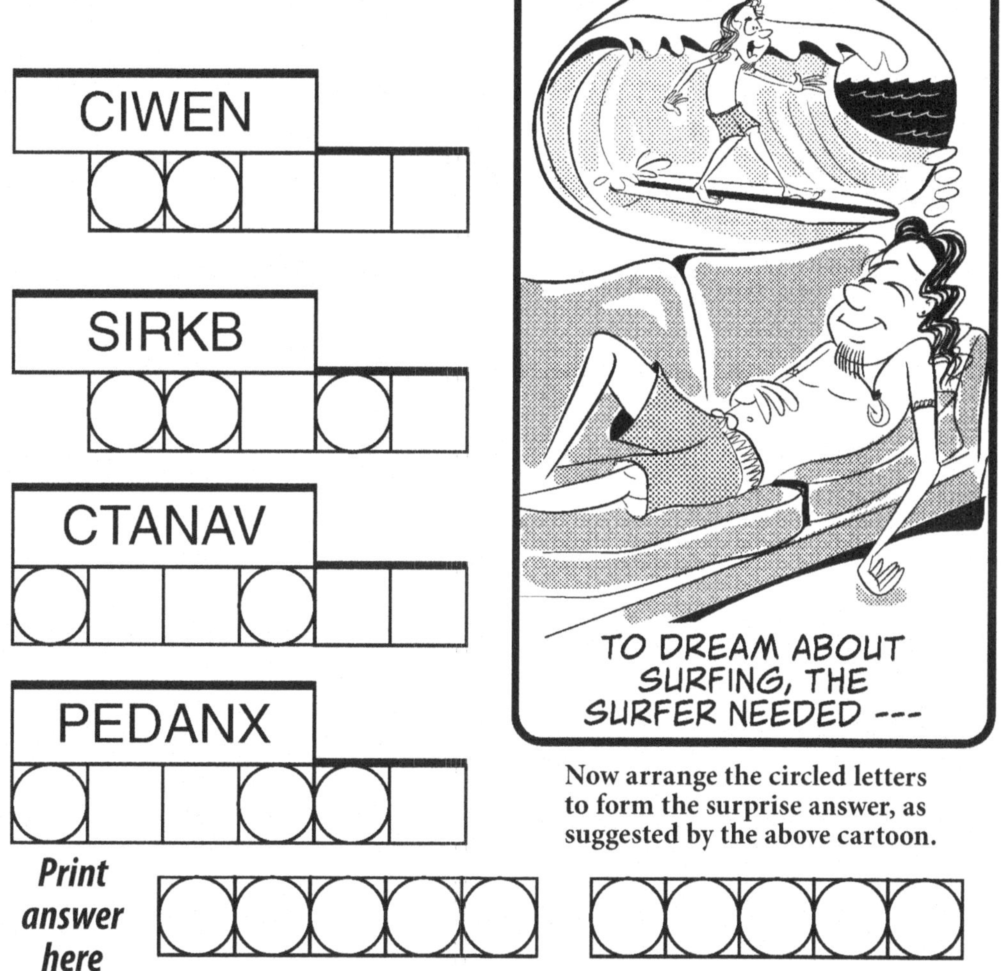
TO DREAM ABOUT SURFING, THE SURFER NEEDED ---

Now arrange the circled letters to form the surprise answer, as suggested by the above cartoon.

Print answer here

PUZZLE
142

JUMBLE®

Unscramble these four Jumbles, one letter to each square, to form four ordinary words.

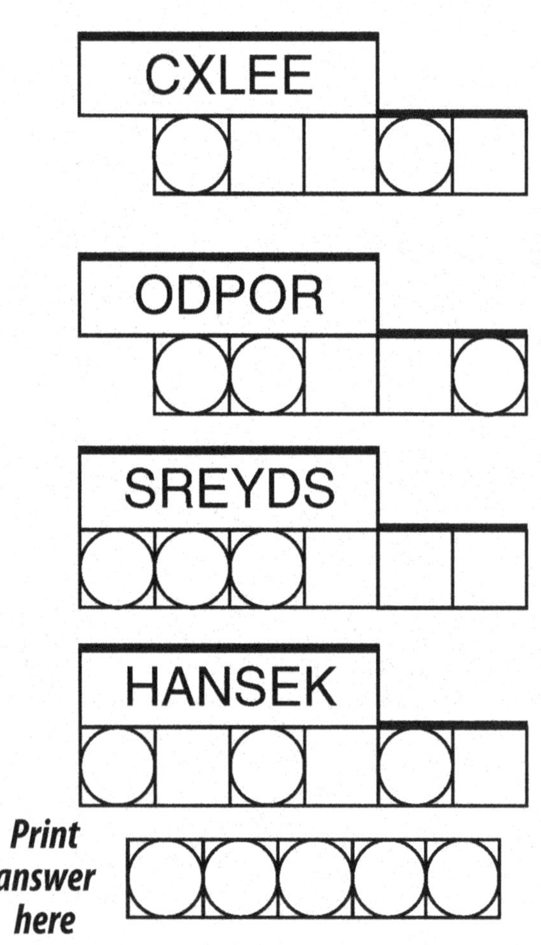

CXLEE
ODPOR
SREYDS
HANSEK
Print answer here

Wow! This has a lot of features.
I breezed through it. I'll tell you about it in the car.
THE POLICEMAN WHO BREEZED THROUGH THE RADAR DETECTOR'S MANUAL WAS A ---

Now arrange the circled letters to form the surprise answer, as suggested by the above cartoon.

PUZZLE
143

JUMBLE®

Unscramble these four Jumbles, one letter to each square, to form four ordinary words.

ESEGE

KIDNY

CALOIS

LIWEVS

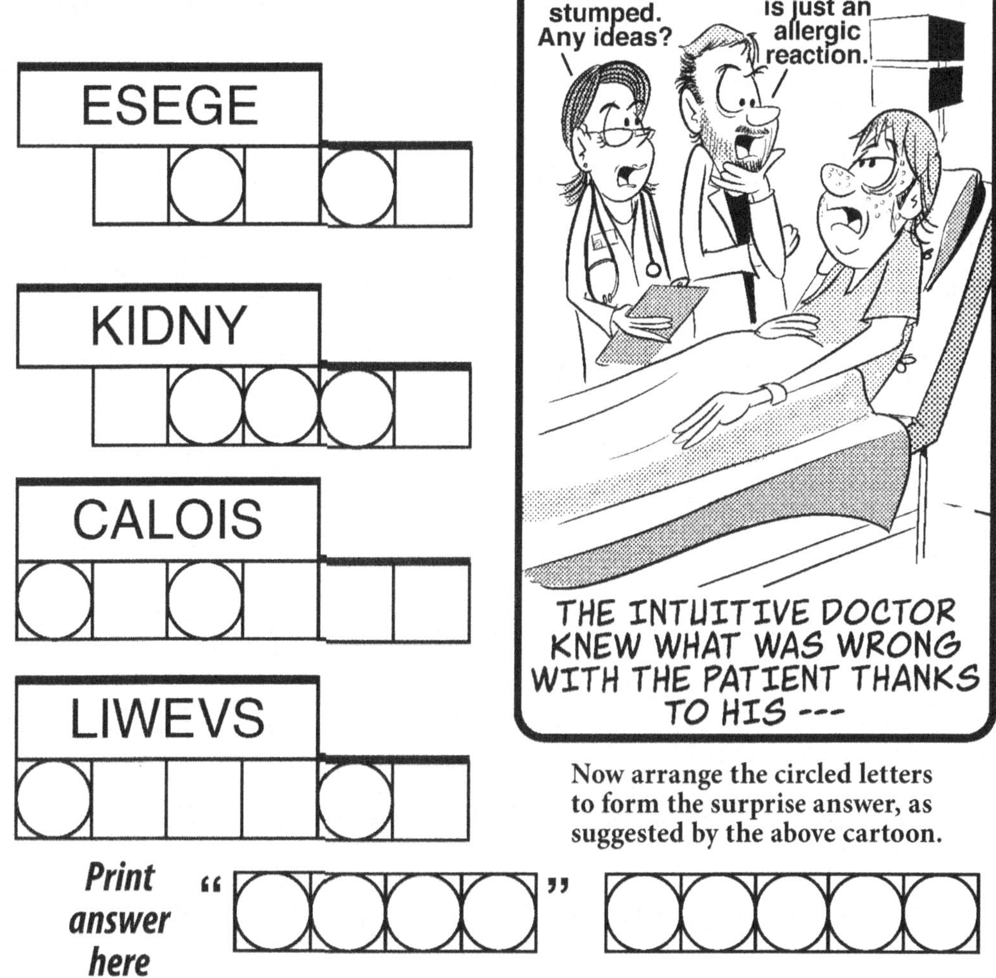
We're all stumped. Any ideas?
I'm feeling this is just an allergic reaction.

THE INTUITIVE DOCTOR KNEW WHAT WAS WRONG WITH THE PATIENT THANKS TO HIS ---

Now arrange the circled letters to form the surprise answer, as suggested by the above cartoon.

Print answer here " "

PUZZLE
144

JUMBLE®
Unscramble these four Jumbles, one letter to each square, to form four ordinary words.
GDAAE
WNIET
TRIUAL
FLEGNU
When I get to the end of a line, I hit this key and it goes back that way.
No one's ever written this way before.
THE AUTHOR SHOWED OFF HIS TYPEWRITER'S DIRECTIONS ---
Now arrange the circled letters to form the surprise answer, as suggested by the above cartoon.
Print answer here
“ ”

PUZZLE
145

JUMBLE®

Unscramble these four Jumbles, one letter to each square, to form four ordinary words.

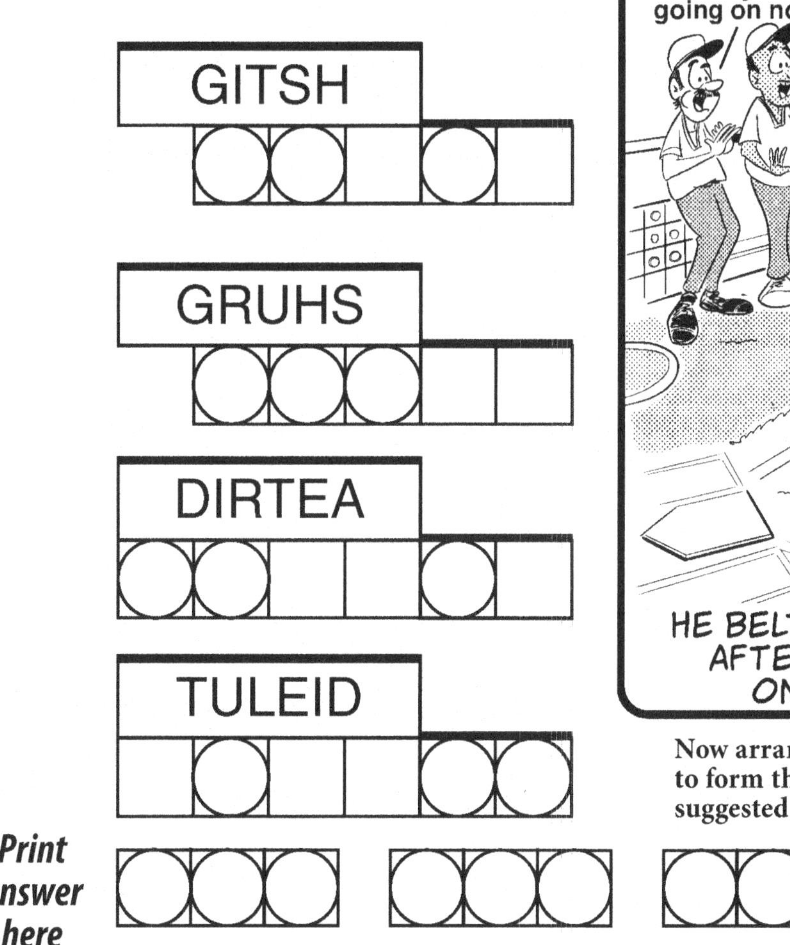
GITSH
GRUHS
DIRTEA
TULEID

After a slow start, he really has it going on now.
I'll say!
HE BELTED HOME RUN AFTER HOME RUN ONCE HE ---

Now arrange the circled letters to form the surprise answer, as suggested by the above cartoon.

Print answer here

PUZZLE
146

JUMBLE®

Unscramble these four Jumbles, one letter to each square, to form four ordinary words.

WHOYD
MURRO
LGOONB
FRATID
Time to fly!
Time to fly!
Time to fly!
NEWS TRAVELED QUICKLY FROM PARROT TO PARROT AS A RESULT OF ---

Now arrange the circled letters to form the surprise answer, as suggested by the above cartoon.

Print answer here " ◯◯◯◯ " ◯◯ ◯◯◯◯◯

PUZZLE
147

JUMBLE®

Unscramble these four Jumbles, one letter to each square, to form four ordinary words.

STEPW

SIPEO

UNERRN

GOUDTU

Someone is enjoying their dinner!
THE CAT'S FAVORITE MEAL WAS ---

Now arrange the circled letters to form the surprise answer, as suggested by the above cartoon.

Print answer here "◯◯◯-◯◯◯◯"

PUZZLE
148

JUMBLE®

Unscramble these four Jumbles, one letter to each square, to form four ordinary words.

RAYWE

BLYUK

REDVUO

BBOECW

I hear it's the best.
Of course it is.
This is incredible!
Wow!
THE NEW SOUP RECIPE AT THE CAFÉ WAS A HUGE HIT. CUSTOMERS WERE ---

Now arrange the circled letters to form the surprise answer, as suggested by the above cartoon.

Print answer here

PUZZLE
149

JUMBLE®

Unscramble these four Jumbles, one letter to each square, to form four ordinary words.

GAVAU

TELUF

NIEAFL

GUTHHO

What do you mean, I wasn't funny?
I heard crickets out there. You're done here.
THE STAND-UP COMEDIAN WAS A HUGE FLOP. IT WOULD BE TOUGH FOR HIM TO ---

Now arrange the circled letters to form the surprise answer, as suggested by the above cartoon.

Print answer here

PUZZLE
150

JUMBLE®

Unscramble these four Jumbles, one letter to each square, to form four ordinary words.

TEERB
SWYNO
ITAXFE
SGRNIT
I thought you used a French press when you wanted coffee quickly?
I do. But crystals are another way to make a fast cup.
QUICK COFFEE
I ♥ JUMBLE
I ♥ JUMBLE
SOME PEOPLE PREFER TO MAKE COFFEE QUICKLY, LIKE USING CRYSTALS ---

Now arrange the circled letters to form the surprise answer, as suggested by the above cartoon.

Print answer here ◯◯◯ "◯◯◯◯◯◯◯◯"

PUZZLE
151

JUMBLE
Unscramble these four Jumbles, one letter to each square, to form four ordinary words.
LITGU
ARKCC
UNORNE
PEANPH
The guy lied at the deli. He said it was salami, but he was full of baloney.
I was going to stuff it in pocket bread, but it was a "pita-ful" excuse for a sandwich.
THE JUMBLE CREATORS' FAVORITE BREAD IS ---
Now arrange the circled letters to form the surprise answer, as suggested by the above cartoon.
Print answer here
" - "

PUZZLE
152

JUMBLE®

Unscramble these four Jumbles, one letter to each square, to form four ordinary words.

SATHS
HNIEW
INDOIE
AGNAME

She did it!
Wow! Her first championship.
Way to go, Syd!
Sydney
"VICTORY" AND "VICTORY" ARE ---

Now arrange the circled letters to form the surprise answer, as suggested by the above cartoon.

Print answer here

PUZZLE
153

JUMBLE®

Unscramble these four Jumbles, one letter to each square, to form four ordinary words.

NAOCG
ROPFO
IOCEOK
TENNYI
I'm so happy I invested in this.
I'm glad you have a slice of it.
SHE INVESTED IN THE PIZZA PARLOR BECAUSE SHE WANTED A ---
Print answer here
THE

Now arrange the circled letters to form the surprise answer, as suggested by the above cartoon.

PUZZLE
154

JUMBLE®

Unscramble these four Jumbles, one letter to each square, to form four ordinary words.

SAUME

MIKPS

SLOJET

POMTIR

Our paths crossing was destiny.
I feel the same way.
HE FELT THAT FATE WAS LEADING HIM TO GIVE HER A SMOOCH. IT WAS ---

Now arrange the circled letters to form the surprise answer, as suggested by the above cartoon.

Print answer here " ____ - ___ "

PUZZLE
155

JUMBLE®
PRETU
VAYHE
NOTGRS
DSWIMO
Our owner loves candy. That's why he started the company.
I thought there'd be more to it.
THE STORY ABOUT THE CANDY FACTORY WAS ---

Unscramble these four Jumbles, one letter to each square, to form four ordinary words.

Now arrange the circled letters to form the surprise answer, as suggested by the above cartoon.

Print answer here

PUZZLE
156

JUMBLE®

Unscramble these four Jumbles, one letter to each square, to form four ordinary words.

ARYIN
CALTH
CEPCAT
VITIEN
When you awaken, the flight will seem like it was only 10 minutes long.
THE HYPNOTIST WHO WORKED IN EUROPE AND NORTH AMERICA WAS---

Now arrange the circled letters to form the surprise answer, as suggested by the above cartoon.

Print answer here “ ” -

PUZZLE
157

JUMBLE®

Unscramble these four Jumbles, one letter to each square, to form four ordinary words.

FINSF

GHTTI

KNARYC

EEGULA

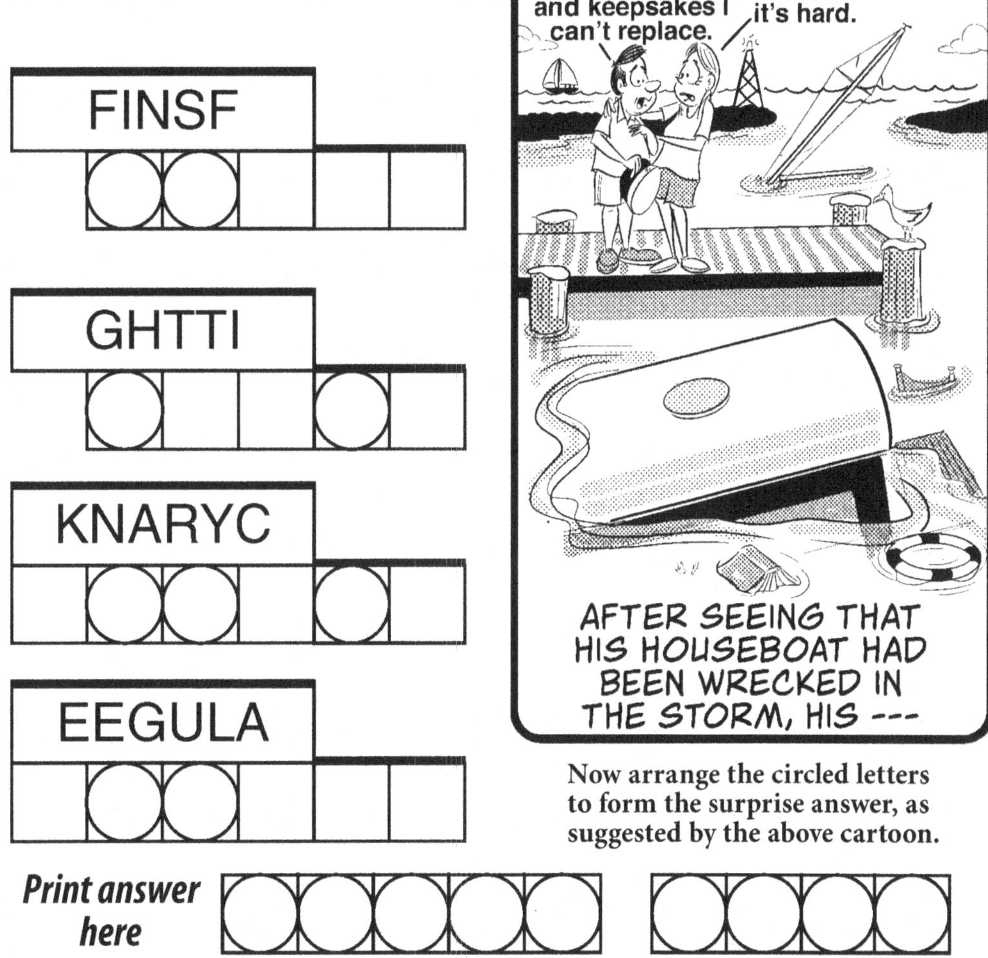
It's the photos and keepsakes I can't replace.
I know it's hard.
AFTER SEEING THAT HIS HOUSEBOAT HAD BEEN WRECKED IN THE STORM, HIS ---

Now arrange the circled letters to form the surprise answer, as suggested by the above cartoon.

Print answer here

PUZZLE
158

JUMBLE®

Unscramble these four Jumbles, one letter to each square, to form four ordinary words.

FEAGF
RNOWS
LASRWU
ZECIRO
You've ruined my outfit! How can I put this on?
HER CAT SLEPT ON HER SWEATER, AND NOW IT WAS ---

Now arrange the circled letters to form the surprise answer, as suggested by the above cartoon.

Print answer here " "

PUZZLE
159

JUMBLE®
Unscramble these four Jumbles, one letter to each square, to form four ordinary words.
PIOHP
NTIHN
RENVIT
ETRTLE
We need to wrap this up. I've got two more projects for you to begin.
I'm trying.
THE OIL COMPANY WAS BEHIND SCHEDULE BECAUSE OF TOO MANY PROJECTS ---
Now arrange the circled letters to form the surprise answer, as suggested by the above cartoon.
Print answer here

PUZZLE
160

JUMBLE®

Unscramble these four Jumbles, one letter to each square, to form four ordinary words.

HVOSE

HMERY

TRAPBU

CNAITT

You know you need to move your body to hula dance, right?
Yes. I saw it on YouTube.
THE TRENDY YOUNG HULA DANCER WAS A ---

Now arrange the circled letters to form the surprise answer, as suggested by the above cartoon.

Print answer here

JUMBLE®
Masterpiece

Challenger Puzzles

PUZZLE
161

JUMBLE®

Unscramble these six Jumbles, one letter to each square, to form six ordinary words.

PUNCOO

ENGLIT

BRANER

QUOPEA

HIRTTY

STUJAD

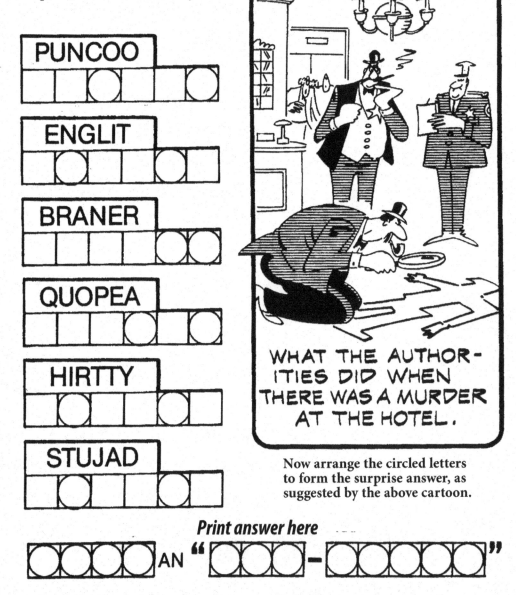

WHAT THE AUTHOR-ITIES DID WHEN THERE WAS A MURDER AT THE HOTEL.

Now arrange the circled letters to form the surprise answer, as suggested by the above cartoon.

Print answer here

AN "___-______"

PUZZLE
162

JUMBLE®

Unscramble these six Jumbles, one letter to each square, to form six ordinary words.

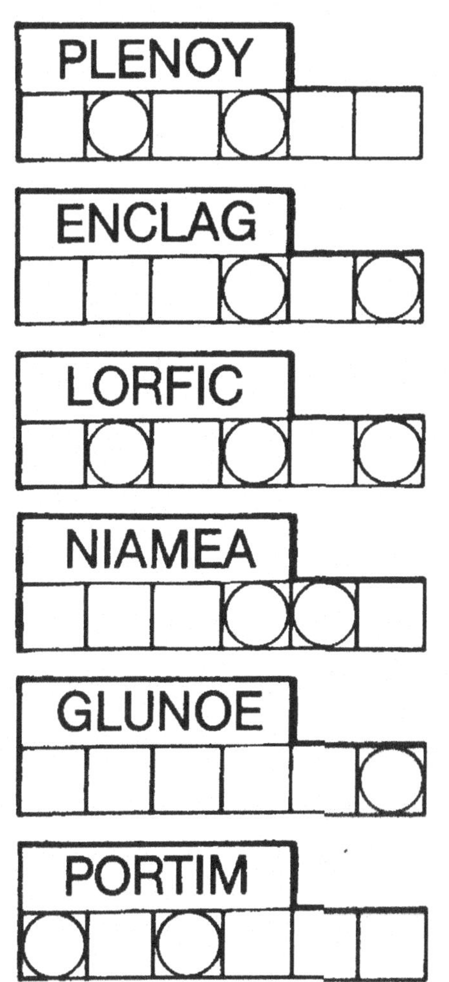

PLENOY
ENCLAG
LORFIC
NIAMEA
GLUNOE
PORTIM

That's Washington, surrounded by Adams, Jefferson and Hamilton
IN GOOD GOVERNMENT, THE PRINCIPAL MEN SHOULD BE THIS.

Now arrange the circled letters to form the surprise answer, as suggested by the above cartoon.

Print answer here

OF

PUZZLE
163

JUMBLE®

Unscramble these six Jumbles, one letter to each square, to form six ordinary words.

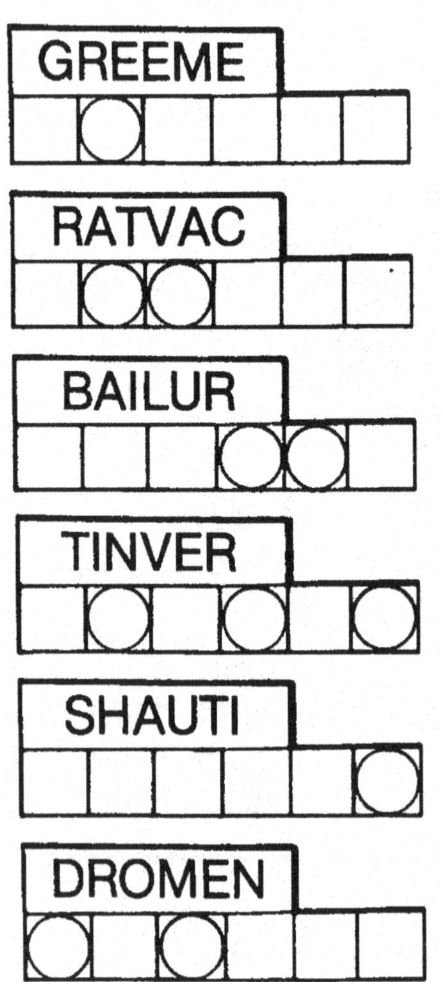
GREEME
RATVAC
BAILUR
TINVER
SHAUTI
DROMEN

WHAT KIND OF A CONFERENCE IS THIS, APPARENTLY?

Now arrange the circled letters to form the surprise answer, as suggested by the above cartoon.

Print answer here

“ ”

PUZZLE
164

JUMBLE®

Unscramble these six Jumbles, one letter to each square, to form six ordinary words.

MEEDER

STAPOL

NAHVIS

TOYBAN

FOISSY

RETORR

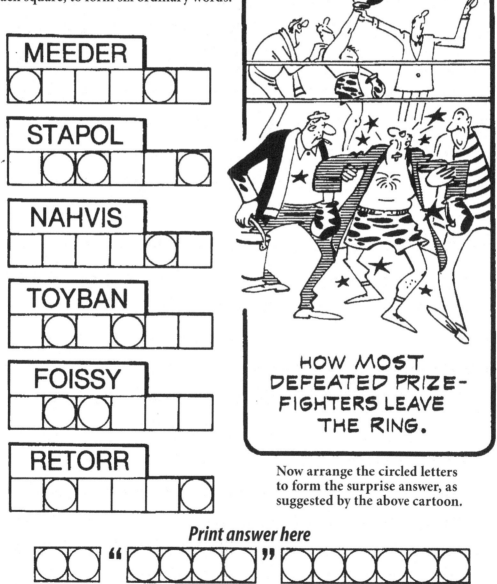

HOW MOST DEFEATED PRIZE-FIGHTERS LEAVE THE RING.

Now arrange the circled letters to form the surprise answer, as suggested by the above cartoon.

Print answer here

“ ”

PUZZLE
165

JUMBLE®

Unscramble these six Jumbles, one letter to each square, to form six ordinary words.

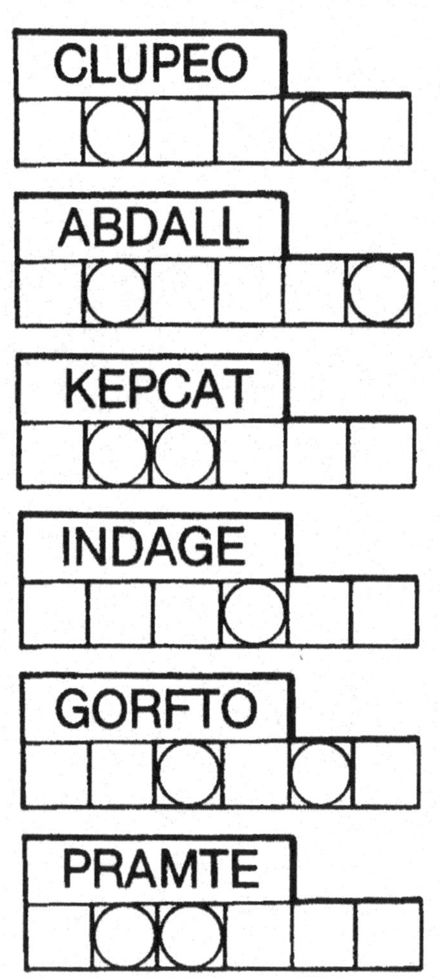
CLUPEO
ABDALL
KEPCAT
INDAGE
GORFTO
PRAMTE

KOFF KOFF
AN EVENING DRESS IS SOMETIMES DE-SIGNED TO HELP THE WEARER CATCH THIS.

Now arrange the circled letters to form the surprise answer, as suggested by the above cartoon.

Print answer here

PUZZLE
166

JUMBLE®

Unscramble these six Jumbles, one letter to each square, to form six ordinary words.

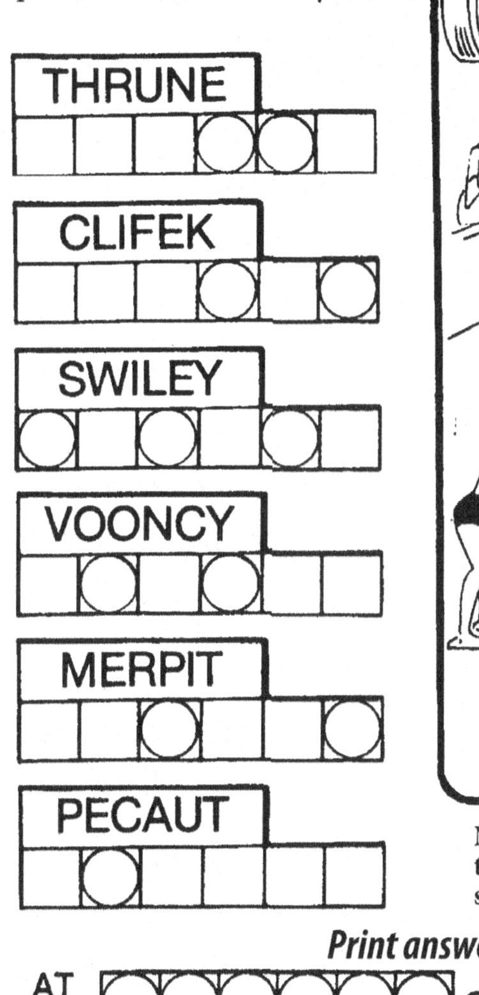
THRUNE
CLIFEK
SWILEY
VOONCY
MERPIT
PECAUT

WHEN DID A DOZEN SWIMMERS TAKE THE PLUNGE?

Now arrange the circled letters to form the surprise answer, as suggested by the above cartoon.

Print answer here

AT THE ◯◯◯◯◯◯◯◯ OF ◯◯◯◯◯◯◯

PUZZLE
167

JUMBLE®

Unscramble these six Jumbles, one letter to each square, to form six ordinary words.

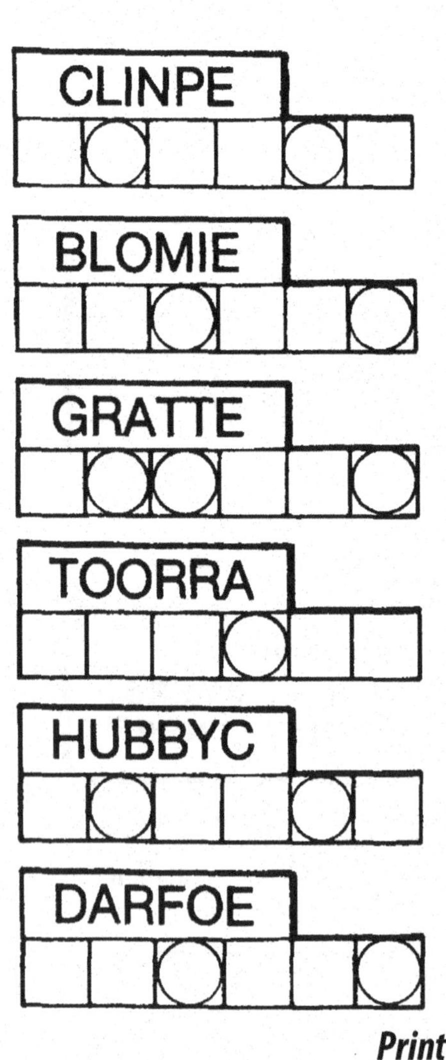

CLINPE
BLOMIE
GRATTE
TOORRA
HUBBYC
DARFOE

?
A CAT ATE CHEESE AND WAITED FOR THE MOUSE WITH THIS.

Now arrange the circled letters to form the surprise answer, as suggested by the above cartoon.

Print answer here

PUZZLE
168

JUMBLE®

Unscramble these six Jumbles, one letter to each square, to form six ordinary words.

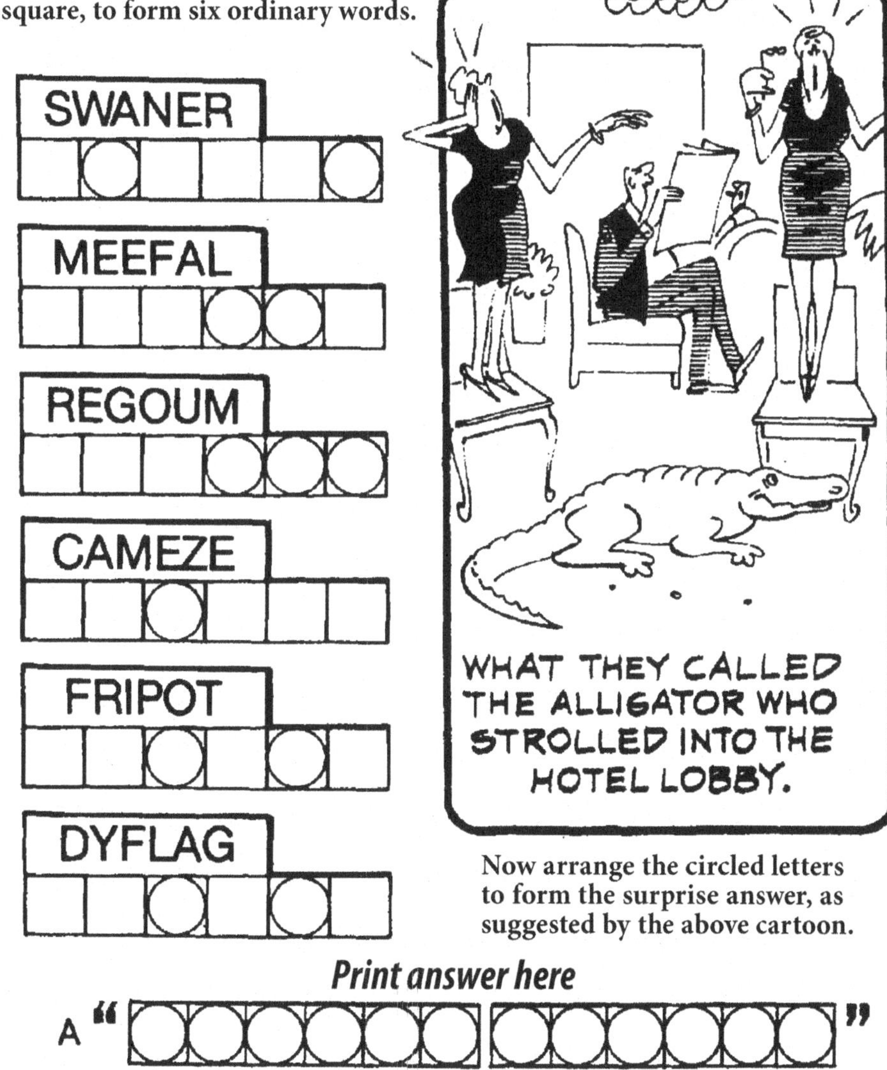
SWANER
MEEFAL
REGOUM
CAMEZE
FRIPOT
DYFLAG
WHAT THEY CALLED THE ALLIGATOR WHO STROLLED INTO THE HOTEL LOBBY.

Now arrange the circled letters to form the surprise answer, as suggested by the above cartoon.

Print answer here

A " "

PUZZLE
169

JUMBLE®

Unscramble these six Jumbles, one letter to each square, to form six ordinary words.

NEEGIN

BOPISH

SHATAM

GEXONY

EXPLUD

FLACIE

WHEN THE LUMBER-JACK WENT INTO TOWN FOR SUPPLIES, HE PUT A NEW AX ON THIS.

Now arrange the circled letters to form the surprise answer, as suggested by the above cartoon.

Print answer here

HIS "◯◯◯◯◯◯◯◯◯" ◯◯◯◯

JUMBLE®

Unscramble these six Jumbles, one letter to each square, to form six ordinary words.

NODARP

YOMARR

BONKER

YEMBOR

LUCASE

GROITE

They're both a couple of dogs as far as I'm concerned

WHAT PRESIDENTIAL "TIMBER" IS OFTEN COMPOSED OF.

Now arrange the circled letters to form the surprise answer, as suggested by the above cartoon.

Print answer here

" "

PUZZLE
171

JUMBLE®

Unscramble these six Jumbles, one letter to each square, to form six ordinary words.

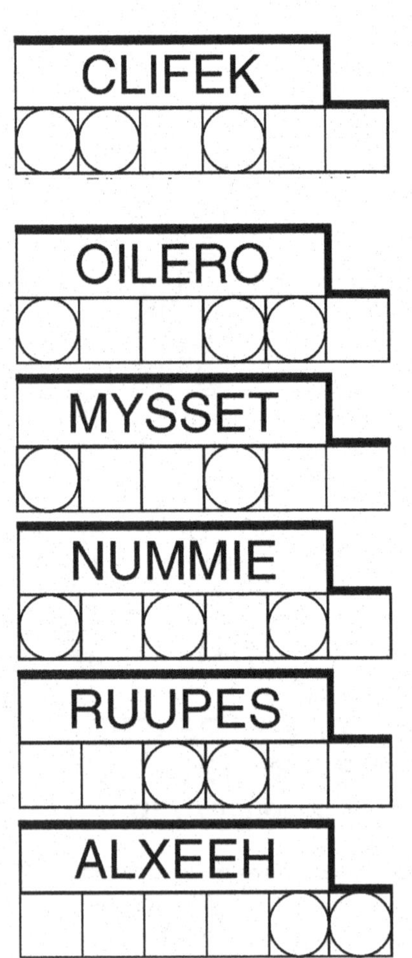
CLIFEK
OILERO
MYSSET
NUMMIE
RUUPES
ALXEEH

How did you get in without removing the engine?
It's like watching a surgeon.
TO BE AN EXPERT MECHANIC REQUIRES ---

Now arrange the circled letters to form the surprise answer, as suggested by the above cartoon.

Print answer here

PUZZLE
172

JUMBLE®

Unscramble these six Jumbles, one letter to each square, to form six ordinary words.

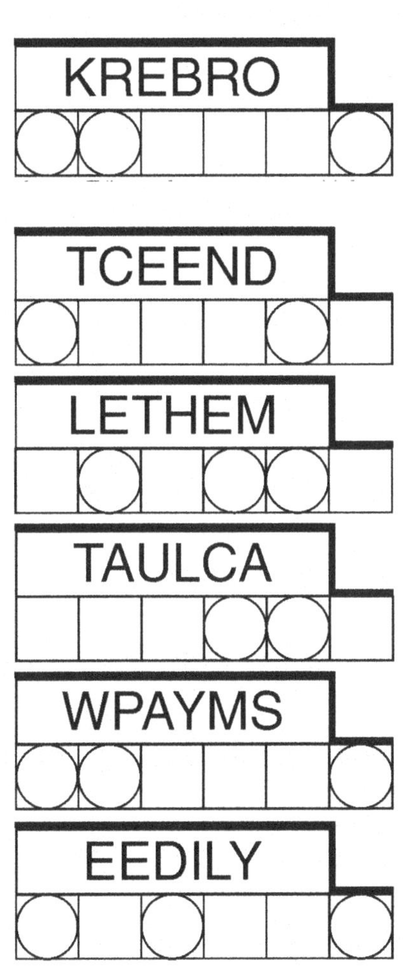

KREBRO
TCEEND
LETHEM
TAULCA
WPAYMS
EEDILY

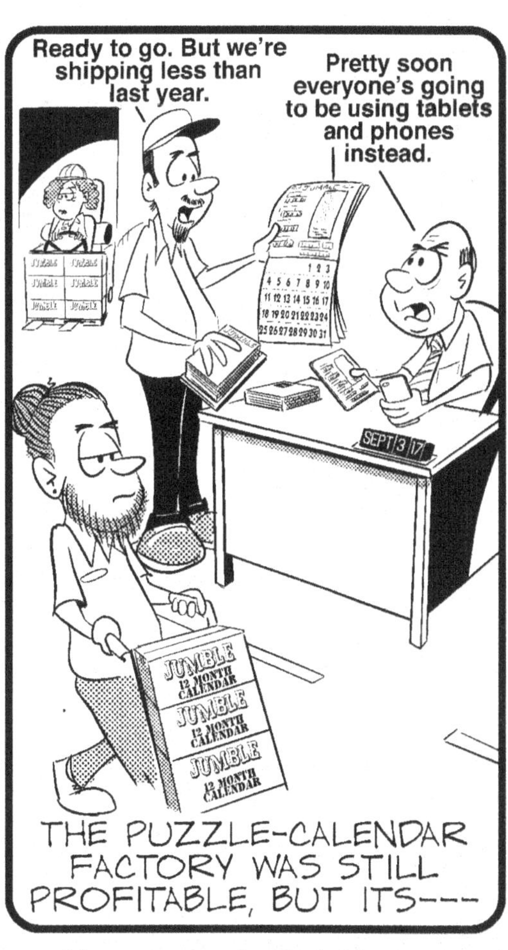

Ready to go. But we're shipping less than last year.
Pretty soon everyone's going to be using tablets and phones instead.
SEPT 3 17
THE PUZZLE-CALENDAR FACTORY WAS STILL PROFITABLE, BUT ITS---

Now arrange the circled letters to form the surprise answer, as suggested by the above cartoon.

Print answer here

PUZZLE
173

JUMBLE®

Unscramble these six Jumbles, one letter to each square, to form six ordinary words.

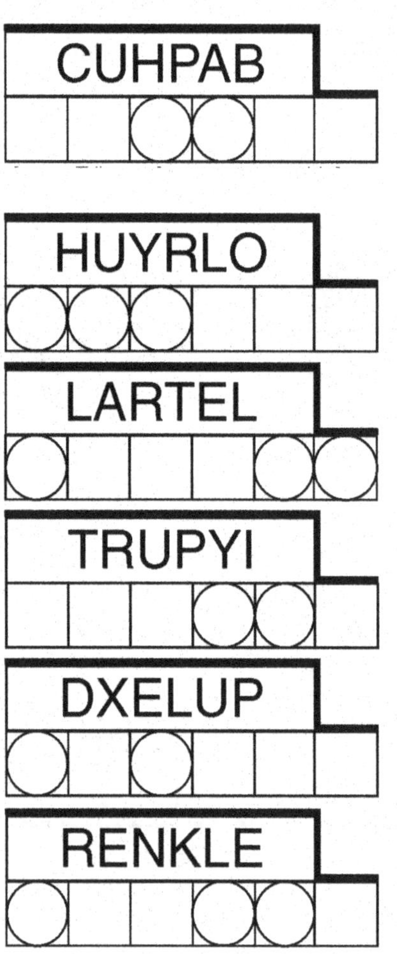
CUHPAB
HUYRLO
LARTEL
TRUPYI
DXELUP
RENKLE

I think we can expand right away.
With 10,000 more acres, we'll be syrup kings.
THE FIRST PROFITS THEY MADE FROM MAPLE SYRUP WERE A ---

Now arrange the circled letters to form the surprise answer, as suggested by the above cartoon.

Print answer here

PUZZLE
174

JUMBLE®

Unscramble these six Jumbles, one letter to each square, to form six ordinary words.

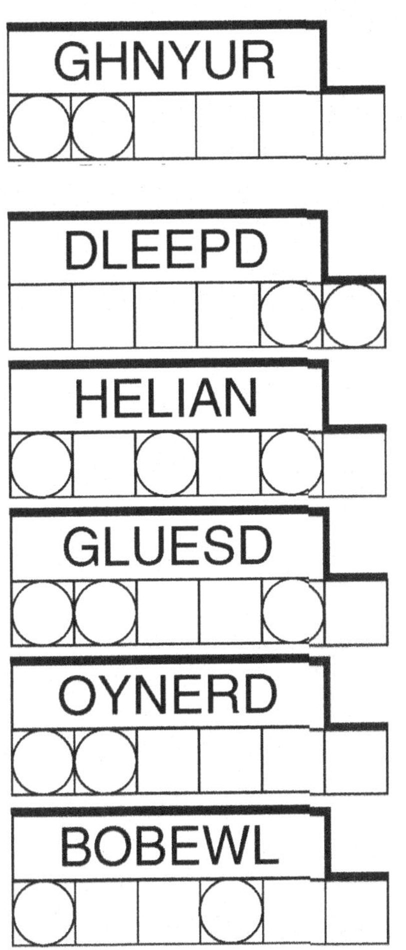
GHNYUR
DLEEPD
HELIAN
GLUESD
OYNERD
BOBEWL

Coming soon
RAVE TOWERS
90 Stories of
Luxury Condos.
I got this land for a steal. The penthouse sales alone will pay for the land.
It's going to be tall.
HE PURCHASED THE LAND TO BUILD THE SKYSCRAPER BECAUSE HE WANTED TO ---

Now arrange the circled letters to form the surprise answer, as suggested by the above cartoon.

Print answer here

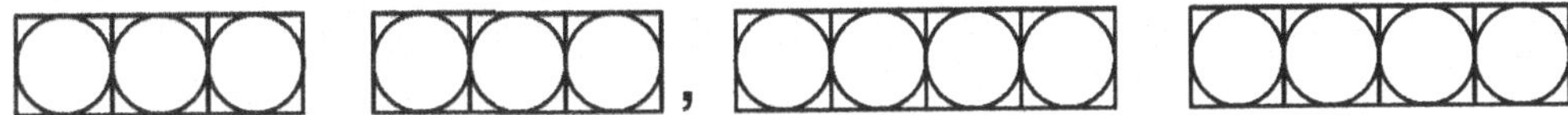

PUZZLE
175

JUMBLE®

Unscramble these six Jumbles, one letter to each square, to form six ordinary words.

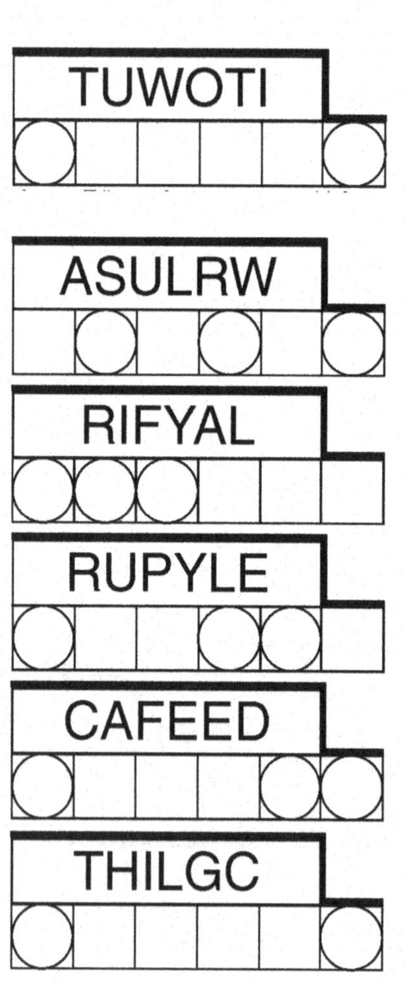
TUWOTI
ASULRW
RIFYAL
RUPYLE
CAFEED
THILGC

I can't believe you dealt me that hand! Sorry I wiped you all out.
I bet you are.
AFTER BEING DEALT A ROYAL FLUSH, THE POKER PLAYER HAD A ---

Now arrange the circled letters to form the surprise answer, as suggested by the above cartoon.

Print answer here

PUZZLE
176

JUMBLE®

Unscramble these six Jumbles, one letter to each square, to form six ordinary words.

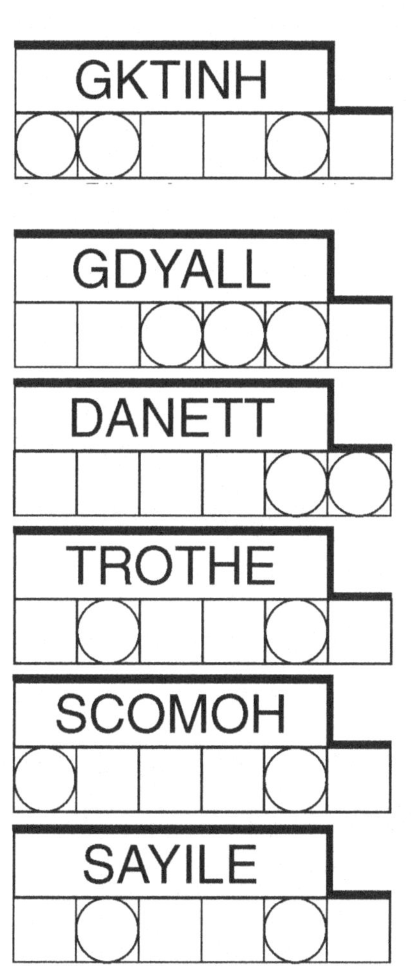
GKTINH
GDYALL
DANETT
TROTHE
SCOMOH
SAYILE

It's nice to have everyone home to help out.
We'll knock this out in no time.
So far, no splinters.
WHEN THE WHOLE FAMILY GOT INVOLVED IN BUILDING AN OUTDOOR LIVING SPACE, IT WAS ---

Now arrange the circled letters to form the surprise answer, as suggested by the above cartoon.

Print answer here

PUZZLE
177

JUMBLE®

Unscramble these six Jumbles, one letter to each square, to form six ordinary words.

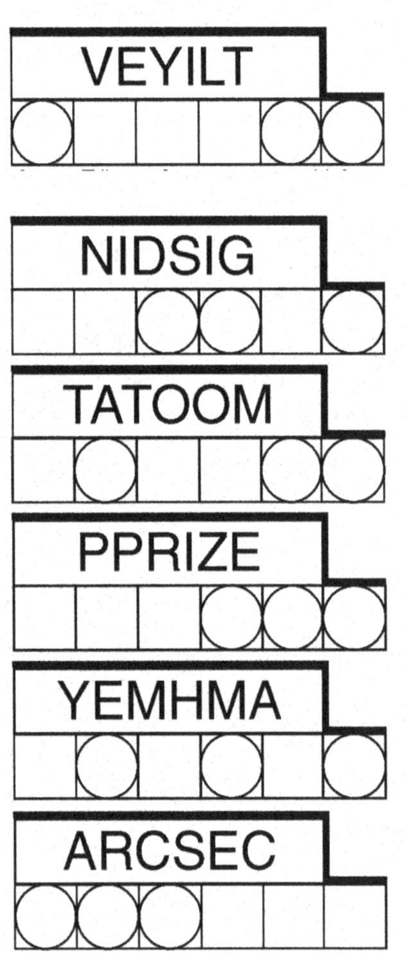
VEYILT
NIDSIG
TATOOM
PPRIZE
YEMHMA
ARCSEC

I thought if anybody could tell us what the rash is from, it would be you.
I've seen this on rhinos and hippos, too.
WHEN THE ELEPHANT DEVELOPED A SKIN PROBLEM, THEY BROUGHT IN A ---

Now arrange the circled letters to form the surprise answer, as suggested by the above cartoon.

Print answer here

PUZZLE
178

JUMBLE®

Unscramble these six Jumbles, one letter to each square, to form six ordinary words.

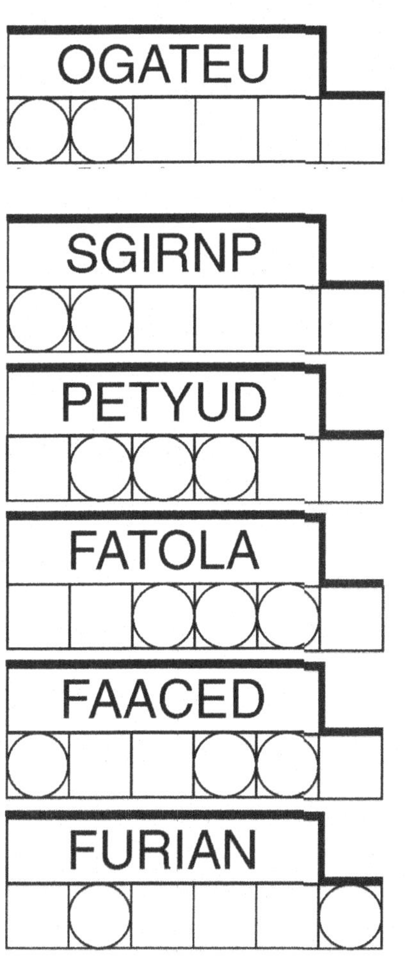
OGATEU
SGIRNP
PETYUD
FATOLA
FAACED
FURIAN

Thank you! You're too kind.
WITH THE AUDIENCE IN A CIRCLE, THE PERFORMER RECEIVED A ---

Now arrange the circled letters to form the surprise answer, as suggested by the above cartoon.

Print answer here

PUZZLE
179

JUMBLE®

Unscramble these six Jumbles, one letter to each square, to form six ordinary words.

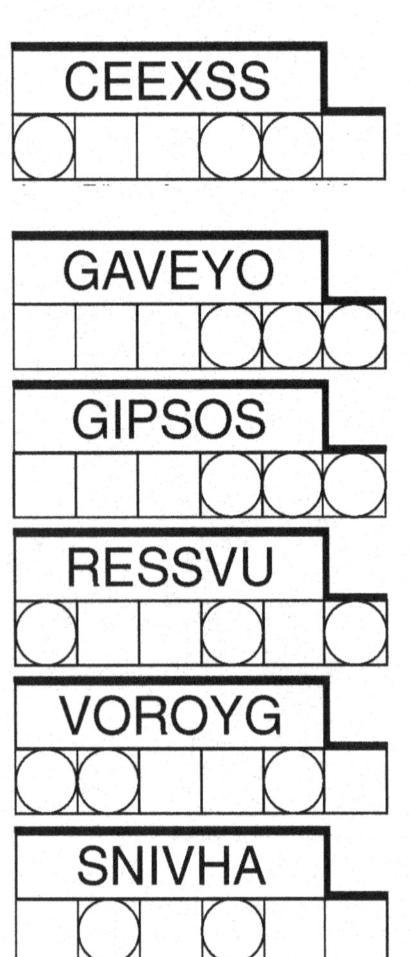

CEEXSS
GAVEYO
GIPSOS
RESSVU
VOROYG
SNIVHA

You know that you're supposed to throw to our team, right?
Your horrible plays are the only things offensive about you.
THE QUARTERBACKS WHO DIDN'T GET ALONG WERE ---

Now arrange the circled letters to form the surprise answer, as suggested by the above cartoon.

Print answer here

PUZZLE
180

JUMBLE®

Unscramble these six Jumbles, one letter to each square, to form six ordinary words.

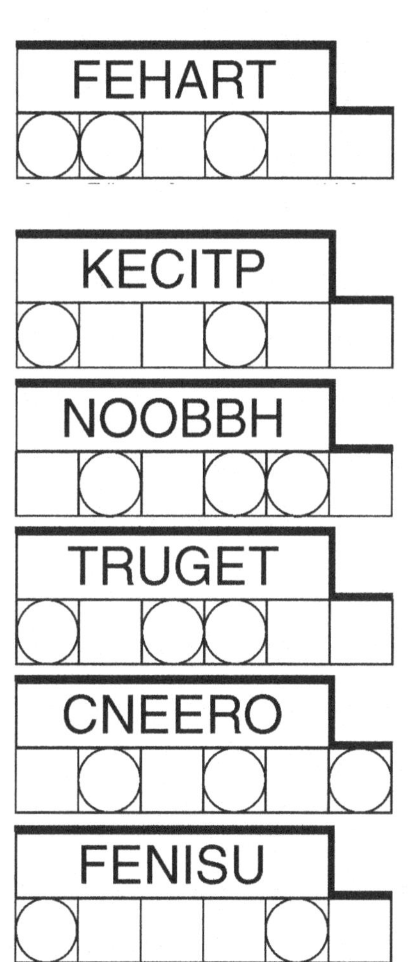
FEHART
KECITP
NOOBBH
TRUGET
CNEERO
FENISU

Can we give him some money?
I have an imaginary dollar right here.
He's good.
I don't like this.
Here's 30¢.

THE PERFORMER EARNED SOME MONEY WORKING AS A MIME, BUT IT WAS ---

Now arrange the circled letters to form the surprise answer, as suggested by the above cartoon.

Print answer here

Answers

1. **Jumbles:** PUPPY FEIGN UNLOCK SLEIGH
Answer: How to make Dracula happy—KEEP YOUR CHIN UP

2. **Jumbles:** BOOTH IRATE SWERVE KIMONO
Answer: He liked the job, but hated this—THE WORK

3. **Jumbles:** USURP CREEK ABDUCT DROWSY
Answer: What a person who spends too much time studying ceramics might end up as—A CRACKPOT

4. **Jumbles:** DANDY TWILL SOCIAL DEVOUR
Answer: What a gambling addict usually is—AT ODDS WITH THE WORLD

5. **Jumbles:** POUND ENSUE STUDIO WISELY
Answer: What the yo-yo business has—ITS UPS & DOWNS

6. **Jumbles:** HENNA ARMOR STOOGE POPLIN
Answer: That conceited guy didn't feel the need for a vacation because he was already on this—A EGO TRIP

7. **Jumbles:** MINER LUCID TUSSLE GIGGLE
Answer: What she said at the costume party—"DIS-GUISE" FOR ME! (This guy's for me)

8. **Jumbles:** CLOVE LAUGH WAITER BLAZER
Answer: A spendthrift wife might love her husband for this—ALL HE'S WORTH

9. **Jumbles:** THICK FEWER BISECT COSTLY
Answer: How a handicapped golfer plays—WITH HIS BOSS

10. **Jumbles:** DECAY TARDY SLOUCH PURPLE
Answer: What an easy talker generally is—A HARD STOPPER

11. **Jumbles:** TRULY BAKED JERSEY NIPPLE
Answer: What the audience gave him when he was expecting cheers—JEERS

12. **Jumbles:** PIECE FEINT THRESH WISDOM
Answer: What a good shrink is supposed to be—A MIND SWEEPER

13. **Jumbles:** PANIC DOUGH UNSOLD GRASSY
Answer: What form of speech is double-talk?—VERY "SINGULAR"

14. **Jumbles:** MOLDY QUAKE SAVAGE BREACH
Answer: What a girl who looked like a million bucks was—JUST AS HARD TO MAKE

15. **Jumbles:** GAUGE LYRIC UPHELD INFORM
Answer: What they called the genealogist—THE "CLAN" DIGGER

16. **Jumbles:** CRAZE YEARN BRIDLE SEETHE
Answer: What nostalgia summons up—"YESTER-DAZE"

17. **Jumbles:** GIVEN AFOOT KITTEN EASILY
Answer: What they called the stingy dermatologist—A SKINFLINT

18. **Jumbles:** BOWER HEFTY DECENT LIMPID
Answer: What a hypochondriac's affliction frequently is—A FICTION

19. **Jumbles:** ADAGE MOUSY STOLEN CARBON
Answer: What he said when the judge sentenced him to be hanged—THAT'S BAD "NOOSE"

20. **Jumbles:** SHEAF FOAMY INLAND OPENLY
Answer: What the egotistical nudist was all wrapped up in—ONLY HIMSELF

21. **Jumbles:** BULGY LATHE JINGLE DISOWN
Answer: What nobility usually is—"SNOB-ILITY"

22. **Jumbles:** CHESS MIRTH SHREWD PITIED
Answer: What a miniskirt is—A "TEMPT-DRESS"

23. **Jumbles:** TUNED GLORY SLOGAN IMBUED
Answer: How that perfume held him—"SMELL-BOUND"

24. **Jumbles:** CLOUT BALMY SINGLE BUTTER
Answer: What you need to have in order to be an organ grinder—A TURN FOR MUSIC

25. **Jumbles:** KITTY LEAVE BAKERY MAGNET
Answer: Where the opera singer's little aria came from—A BIG "AREA"

26. **Jumbles:** DOUBT KNOWN EXCITE JOVIAL
Answer: What the bus driver said—"JACK" IN THE BOX!

27. **Jumbles:** CATCH LYING GENIUS VANISH
Answer: What there was plenty of at the penthouse—HIGH LIVING

28. **Jumbles:** WOMEN PECAN HALVED GUTTER
Answer: What those talkative moths did—CHEWED THE RAG

29. **Jumbles:** WEIGH BEGUN PLENTY BUREAU
Answer: How some frank people make their point—BY BEING BLUNT

30. **Jumbles:** RAINY CUBIT LOCATE DOUBLY
Answer: Tired of looking at all those roadside ads—"BILL-BORED"

31. **Jumbles:** PARKA TOXIC DROPSY ACCORD
Answer: What a person who spends every afternoon watching TV undoubtedly is—A "SOAP" ADDICT

32. **Jumbles:** BANJO PROVE DIVIDE ZENITH
Answer: What the hula dancer did to the guys in the audience—"HIP-NOTIZED" 'EM

33. **Jumbles:** QUILT GORGE SHAKEN BLOUSE
Answer: Why they always accused him of being negative—HE WAS A "NO-IT-ALL"

34. **Jumbles:** MIDGE NUTTY CRAYON BUSHEL
Answer: What her steady date was much of the time—UNSTEADY

35. **Jumbles:** LIMBO BRAWL FUTURE PYTHON
Answer: When it comes to a dishwasher, most every husband would rather do this—BUY THAN BE

36. **Jumbles:** COVEY DIZZY KNIGHT HAZARD
Answer: What all that talk about horoscopes was—"ZODI-YAK"

37. **Jumbles:** MINCE EXPEL ANEMIA WIDEST
Answer: A counterfeiter is the only man in the world who makes more money than this—ANYONE CAN SPEND

38. **Jumbles:** SNOWY EMERY DETAIN GOITER
Answer: What a globe-trotter had—A "ROAMIN'" NOSE

39. **Jumbles:** CHIME GLAND FALLEN BEAVER
Answer: Jealousy sets in with the arrival of this—A RIVAL

40. **Jumbles:** CURRY PIOUS DECADE SALUTE
Answer: How careless drivers frequently end up—"CARLESS"

41. **Jumbles:** GNOME SHAKY CLAUSE DECEIT
Answer: The "go-getter" knows that the rules for getting ahead won't work unless this happens—<u>HE</u> DOES

42. **Jumbles:** BATCH ELATE DELUGE CURFEW
Answer: What that "go-getter" finally managed to do—"GET HER"

43. **Jumbles:** IRONY WAGER BEHOLD FARINA
Answer: What accordion music might sometimes be—LONG DRAWN OUT

44. **Jumbles:** PANDA MINOR DONKEY FIERCE
Answer: Where can you buy camel's milk?—AT A "DROME-DAIRY"

45. **Jumbles:** GASSY CLUCK ASTRAY DEVICE
Answer: A glutton often eats more than at other times but seldom this—LESS

46. **Jumbles:** PANSY DUMPY FRUGAL JOCKEY
Answer: What she said about that disappointing letter carrier—JUNK "MALE"!

47. **Jumbles:** QUEST GAWKY DENOTE SURELY
Answer: What to wear when working outdoors—A "LAWN DRESS"

48. **Jumbles:** POKED HONOR GULLET FAMISH
Answer: What a visitor to Hawaii is interested in finding out about first—THE "LEI" OF THE LAND

49. **Jumbles:** BEIGE PEONY DISCUS FORGET
Answer: What a murky fog gives drivers—THE "CREEPS"

50. **Jumbles:** QUEEN FACET KILLER NIPPLE
Answer: What nepotism is—"KIN-FLUENCE"

51. **Jumbles:** KNAVE UNWED JUNIOR WOBBLE
Answer: What an artist's model doesn't always feel—IN THE "NUDE" FOR WORK

52. **Jumbles:** PRIZE DALLY LIKELY WINNOW
Answer: A legacy is one way of proving that poverty can be overcome by this—"WILL POWER"

53. **Jumbles:** CHAFF SUEDE HERMIT LOUNGE
Answer: What the soprano's "solo" was—"SO HIGH"

54. **Jumbles:** COUPE FORGO INTENT LOCKET
Answer: Always the center of attention—THE LETTER N

55. **Jumbles:** NEWSY SHOWY FIDDLE SATIRE
Answer: She began to call him by his first name when she was after this—HIS LAST

56. **Jumbles:** SWAMP ELEGY DEPUTY BABOON
Answer: A loafer is always ready to do this, to say the least—THE LEAST

57. **Jumbles:** OZONE TABOO GRIMLY RADIUM
Answer: They were participants in a shotgun wedding—THE BRIDE & "GLOOM"

58. **Jumbles:** IVORY BRIAR WHITEN SOCKET
Answer: The fireman is just about the only civil servant you'd prefer to see this way—<u>NOT</u> AT WORK

59. **Jumbles:** ONION SOGGY VASSAL NEWEST
Answer: What a philanderer thinks the world does—OWES HIM A LOVING

60. **Jumbles:** MONEY EXTOL UPLIFT LIZARD
Answer: They called the comedian a "gas," because he was this—JUST AN OLD "FUEL"

61. **Jumbles:** YOUTH PIETY BECKON FAMOUS
Answer: What to exercise when you feel you're putting on weight—CAUTION

62. **Jumbles:** GLEAM UPPER ISLAND EIGHTY
Answer: What that twice-married swine could have been—A "PIG-AMIST"

63. **Jumbles:** Print AMITY FEMALE HAIRDO
Answer: Talks without giving itself away—MONEY

64. **Jumbles:** EXERT FETCH WALNUT HERALD
Answer: What a rainy day is for a cabdriver—"FARE" WEATHER

65. **Jumbles:** QUASH ARBOR GAIETY CLOTHE
Answer: What the zookeeper said his life was—"BEASTLY"

66. **Jumbles:** STEED ARDOR SCARCE RELISH
Answer: What Samson was after Delilah cut off all his hair—"DIS-TRESSED"

67. **Jumbles:** CRACK DADDY GIMLET BOYISH
Answer: What the tax collector did for the man who thought he was saving up for a rainy day—"SOAKED" HIM

68. **Jumbles:** OXIDE LUNGE PURVEY RACIAL
Answer: What milk is for a cat—THE "LAP" OF LUXURY

69. **Jumbles:** DROOP OLDER MUSEUM LOCALE
Answer: How some so-called "music" that's being composed these days sounds to some people—"DE-COMPOSED"

70. **Jumbles:** BRAVE PAPER HAWKER FATHOM
Answer: What his wife's mom turned out to be—A "MOTHER-IN-AWE"

71. **Jumbles:** TARRY FUDGE PIGPEN MORTAR
Answer: The bacteriologist made his famous discovery by starting out with this—THE GERM OF AN IDEA

72. **Jumbles:** JUROR GRAIN KETTLE HECTIC
Answer: A girl wears a girdle to take her in, so that a man will do this—TAKE HER OUT

73. **Jumbles:** VALET DITTY BUNION QUENCH
Answer: What he did after stealing a pair of scissors—"CUT OUT"

74. **Jumbles:** MANGY VILLA FONDLY COMPEL
Answer: A guy who's busy coping has no time for this—MOPING

75. **Jumbles:** KETCH SWISH DEBTOR IRONIC
Answer: What the fisherman turned TV executive knew how to make—THE "NET" WORK

76. **Jumbles:** SWOON ABOUT ECZEMA JETSAM
Answer: What the practical joker had—A ZEST FOR LIFE

77. **Jumbles:** SHINY EPOCH GIGOLO NOUGAT
Answer: With the deadbeat, it's often a matter of this—TOUCH & GO

78. **Jumbles:** CHASM FORCE CAMPER TRUANT
Answer: He was hoping to get his trim figure back, but actually had this—A FAT CHANCE

79. **Jumbles:** AFTER IMPEL MUFFIN TWINGE
Answer: What a blizzard might do to daily life—"WINTER-UPT" IT

80. **Jumbles:** DITTO LOONY EXHALE GAINEDn
Answer: What they were doing at the sewing circle—NEEDLING

81. **Jumbles:** THYME RATIO KARATE BUREAU
Answer: After scuba diving for hours, they were ready to—TAKE A BREATHER

82. **Jumbles:** EXCEL CLAMP OPPOSE EXEMPT
Answer: The new apartment buildings were very confusing. It was a—COMPLEX COMPLEX

83. **Jumbles:** MIGHT FAINT BUCKLE NUMBER
Answer: They drove at 60 MPH, and his annoying passenger was talking a—MILE A MINUTE

84. **Jumbles:** OPERA FACET GROUCH TIMELY
Answer: The chickens were tired of life on the farm and wanted to—FLY THE COOP

85. **Jumbles:** PLANK AWAKE SOOTHE BUDGET
Answer: When the ox-like antelope met up with his friends, he said—WHAT'S "GNU"?

86. **Jumbles:** OCTET HILLY PICKLE STICKY
Answer: In 1908, George Smith, claiming he invented the modern-style lollipop, sold them—LICKETY-SPLIT

87. **Jumbles:** OMEGA PHOTO INNING SPRUCE
Answer: The designers of the single-person blimps were experiencing—ONE-UPMANSHIP

88. **Jumbles:** CARGO SHOVE COTTON PRIMER
Answer: The plastic surgeon who was known for leaving no scars was a—SMOOTH OPERATOR

89. **Jumbles:** KHAKI ROUND PEBBLE BRUNCH
Answer: When the all-star pitcher was presented with a new contract, he—BALKED

90. **Jumbles:** PIANO KAZOO HUMBLE STRAND
Answer: She was shopping for just the right knife and was keeping a—SHARP LOOKOUT

91. **Jumbles:** WEDGE BULKY EYELID CANYON
Answer: The pianist played for just a few people. His performance was—LOW-KEY

92. **Jumbles:** SPOIL CLASH COMEDY INVOKE
Answer: Big Ben was being constructed by workers who had—CLOCKED IN

93. **Jumbles:** UNFIT SENSE COUSIN IODINE
Answer: The conversation between the prison inmates was made possible because of—SENTENCES

94. **Jumbles:** SPELL OOMPH RHYTHM INFLUX
Answer: The baseball player loved his treadmill and all the—HOME RUNS

95. **Jumbles:** KAYAK CABLE CEMENT GROGGY
Answer: The railroad hired a new CEO to help get its business—BACK ON TRACK

96. **Jumbles:** REBEL TREND VENDOR CUSTOM
Answer: The fact that they were tubing down the river now made it a—CURRENT EVENT

97. **Jumbles:** GRUNT BASIS EFFECT DAINTY
Answer: The home run didn't surprise the hitter one bit. He did it without—BATTING AN EYE

98. **Jumbles:** DECAY EVENT WHOOSH POPLAR
Answer: After an exhausting day of frightening people, the legendary horseman was a—SLEEPY HEAD

99. **Jumbles:** VILLA GIZMO CIRCUS HERMIT
Answer: When it came to making things disappear, the illusionist had the—MAGIC TOUCH

100. **Jumbles:** ABOVE HEFTY ADRIFT WICKER
Answer: When asked if she wanted a ring made of gold or silver, she said—EITHER "ORE"

101. **Jumbles:** PAUSE SKUNK TATTOO WALLOP
Answer: They were able to get away from the porcupine because the porcupine was a —SLOWPOKE

102. **Jumbles:** DEPTH DWELL PAPAYA PACIFY
Answer: The telemarketers would work until they—CALLED IT A DAY

103. **Jumbles:** OZONE FLUFF RUNNER ONWARD
Answer: When each of them hit onto the next fairway, the golfers were—"FORE" FOR FOUR

104. **Jumbles:** RUMMY BLEND SPOTTY INDOOR
Answer: Thanks to the success of his firewood business, the owner had—MONEY TO BURN

105. **Jumbles:** STASH SOUPY MEDLEY IMPALA
Answer: They said "hello" as their boats passed each other on the—"HI" SEAS

106. **Jumbles:** TOTAL DEPTH LUXURY JARGON
Answer: After their coffee grinder broke, business at the coffee shop—GROUND TO A HALT

107. **Jumbles:** SWISH DRESS SHREWD OBJECT
Answer: The confusion between the electricians was a result of them getting their—WIRES CROSSED

108. **Jumbles:** GLAZE AWAIT PARDON MEDIUM
Answer: To create the painting of the hog, the artist needed just the right—PIGMENT

109. **Jumbles:** SHAKY APART TRICKY INJECT
Answer: To promote his business, the locksmith wore—"KHA-KEY" PANTS

110. **Jumbles:** OUTDO GUMBO PILLOW DENTAL
Answer: The twins got in trouble a lot. They were often—UP "TWO" NO GOOD

111. **Jumbles:** GLORY UPPER EXODUS OXYGEN
Answer: The farmer viewed his field of pumpkins. To him, it was—"GOURD-GEOUS"

112. **Jumbles:** HOBBY HOIST JAGUAR INTENT
Answer: The boxing match hadn't started yet, but it was—"A-BOUT" TO BEGIN

113. **Jumbles:** BOSSY TARDY ABACUS CASHEW
Answer: For the smart child, learning to put things in alphabetical order was—AS EASY AS A, B, C

114. **Jumbles:** CANAL GOOEY STRONG SWITCH
Answer: When asked what inspired him to write a lengthy book, J.R.R. Tolkien said—IT'S A LONG STORY

115. **Jumbles:** DRESS FRONT PUBLIC SONATA
Answer: The ram refused to smash horns with the other ram—NO IFS, ANDS, OR BUTTS

116. **Jumbles:** GAMUT CABIN SHRANK CELERY
Answer: For safety's sake, the coal-company owners agreed to make some—"MINER" CHANGES

117. **Jumbles:** PRUNE ABIDE sAFEty MUTINY
Answer: If politicians worked together to solve problems, then they could say—BYE-PARTISAN

118. **Jumbles:** BEGUN HOUSE SHRIMP INVENT
Answer: The teacher was explaining action words to the students and was being—VERBOSE

119. **Jumbles:** SPURN IMPEL HEALTH BEFORE
Answer: He really wanted to say hello to the woman and had—"HI" HOPES

120. **Jumbles:** THICK WOUND WARMLY BEHAVE
Answer: When the farmer's baler malfunctioned, things—WENT HAYWIRE

121. **Jumbles:** CROAK SIXTY KERNEL RATHER
Answer: The stone wall would eventually get finished, in spite of the—ROCKY START

122. **Jumbles:** DITTO FRESH ABOUND BEMOAN
Answer: When Velcro was invented, people were—"FASTEN-ATED"

123. **Jumbles:** SHYLY DOUBT HANDLE SLEIGH
Answer: The Scottish Highlands' land formations are as—OLD AS THE HILLS

124. **Jumbles:** ELUDE DERBY BRIGHT FILTHY
Answer: When the storm knocked out power to the school, the students were—"DE-LIGHTED"

125. **Jumbles:** ENVOY QUEST AUTUMN PLEDGE
Answer: The comedian was well-respected. Everyone considered him to be a—STAND-UP GUY

126. **Jumbles:** AWARD CHURN SKETCH ENROLL
Answer: She kept her gloves by the front door so they would be—CLOSE AT HAND

127. **Jumbles:** MAMBO BUDDY RITUAL UNLESS
Answer: They didn't like running at the health club. To them, the machine was a—"DREAD-MILL"

128. **Jumbles:** PANTS UNITY PARADE INDUCT
Answer: The successful software developer had a natural—"APP-TITUDE"

129. **Jumbles:** PROVE CROSS EXPOSE JALOPY
Answer: He sank the winning three-point shot in front of—SCORES OF PEOPLE

130. **Jumbles:** MANLY DOILY FORGET ROTATE
Answer: They spent the day with their daughter's children and had a—GRAND TIME

131. **Jumbles:** MONEY DIGIT GRITTY QUENCH
Answer: With each tentacle holding food, the octopus—"EIGHT" HIS DINNER

132. **Jumbles:** ROYAL BUNCH SEASON SHOULD
Answer: The woodwind player went fishing with his buddy and hoped to catch a—BASS SOON

133. **Jumbles:** SPURN TEASE FALLEN UNEASY
Answer: Track star Usain Bolt dreamed of breaking records when he was—FAST ASLEEP

134. **Jumbles:** GLOAT HAIRY PULPIT EQUATE
Answer: After acing the math test, her parents asked how she did, and she answered—ALL RIGHT

135. **Jumbles:** ISSUE DIMLY THRILL FLABBY
Answer: The painting of the moonshiner's equipment was a—STILL LIFE

136. **Jumbles:** ALBUM APPLY SHABBY UNPAID
Answer: The future eye doctors were—PUPILS

137. **Jumbles:** FLOSS SCOUR RODENT INFLUX
Answer: The golfer's tee shot ended up in a yard as a result of it being hit—OFF COURSE

138. **Jumbles:** ICING SKIMP INVITE NOODLE
Answer: You can buy shares of IBM because the exchange has plenty—IN STOCK

139. **Jumbles:** INEPT KNELT IMPACT NOTARY
Answer: The marsupial couple vacationed together to get some—"KOALA-TY" TIME

140. **Jumbles:** ANNUL BLEAK DAMAGE SCREWY
Answer: There's a Jumble cartoon each day because the artist has never—DRAWN A BLANK

141. **Jumbles:** WINCE BRISK VACANT EXPAND
Answer: To dream about surfing, the surfer needed—BRAIN WAVES

142. **Jumbles:** EXCEL DROOP DRESSY SHAKEN
Answer: The policeman who breezed through the radar detector's manual was a—SPEED READER

143. **Jumbles:** GEESE DINKY SOCIAL SWIVEL
Answer: The intuitive doctor knew what was wrong with the patient thanks to his—"SICK" SENSE

144. **Jumbles:** ADAGE TWINE RITUAL ENGULF
Answer: The author showed off his typewriter's directions—LEFT AND "WRITE"

145. **Jumbles:** SIGHT SHRUG TIRADE DILUTE
Answer: He belted home run after home run once he—HIT HIS STRIDE

146. **Jumbles:** HOWDY RUMOR OBLONG ADRIFT
Answer: News traveled quickly from parrot to parrot as a result of—"BIRD" OF MOUTH

147. **Jumbles:** SWEPT POISE RUNNER DUGOUT
Answer: The cat's favorite meal was—"SUP-PURR"

148. **Jumbles:** WEARY BULKY DEVOUR COBWEB
Answer: The new soup recipe at the café was a huge hit. Customers were—BOWLED OVER

149. **Jumbles:** GUAVA FLUTE FINALE THOUGH
Answer: The stand-up comedian was a huge flop. It would be tough for him to—LAUGH IT OFF

150. **Jumbles:** BERET SNOWY FIXATE STRING
Answer: Some people prefer to make coffee quickly, like using crystals—FOR "INSTANTS"

151. **Jumbles:** GUILT CRACK NEURON HAPPEN
Answer: The Jumble creators' favorite bread is—"PUN-PERNICKLE"

152. **Jumbles:** STASH WHINE IODINE MANAGE
Answer: "Victory" and "victory" are—"WON" AND THE SAME

153. **Jumbles:** CONGA PROOF COOKIE NINETY
Answer: She invested in the pizza parlor because she wanted a—PIECE OF THE ACTION

154. **Jumbles:** AMUSE SKIMP JOSTLE IMPORT
Answer: He felt that fate was leading him to give her a smooch. It was—"KISS-MET"

155. **Jumbles:** ERUPT HEAVY STRONG WISDOM
Answer: The story about the candy factory was—SHORT AND SWEET

156. **Jumbles:** RAINY LATCH ACCEPT INVITE
Answer: The hypnotist who worked in Europe and North America was—"TRANCE"-ATLANTIC

157. **Jumbles:** SNIFF TIGHT CRANKY LEAGUE
Answer: After seeing that his houseboat had been wrecked in the storm, his—HEART SANK

158. **Jumbles:** GAFFE SWORN WALRUS COZIER
Answer: Her cat slept on her sweater, and now it was—WORSE "FUR" WEAR

159. **Jumbles:** HIPPO NINTH INVERT LETTER
Answer: The oil company was behind schedule because of too many projects—IN THE PIPELINE

160. **Jumbles:** SHOVE RHYME ABRUPT INTACT
Answer: The trendy young hula dancer was a—HIPSTER

161. **Jumbles:** COUPON TINGLE BARREN OPAQUE THIRTY ADJUST
Answer: What the authorities did when there was a murder at the hotel—HELD AN "INN-QUEST"

162. **Jumbles:** OPENLY GLANCE FROLIC ANEMIA LOUNGE IMPORT
Answer: In good government, the principal men should be this—MEN OF PRINCIPLE

163. **Jumbles:** EMERGE CRAVAT BURIAL INVERT HIATUS MODERN
Answer: What kind of a conference is this, apparently? —"DISARMAMENT"

164. **Jumbles:** REDEEM POSTAL VANISH BOTANY OSSIFY TERROR
Answer: How most defeated prize-fighters leave the ring—AS "SORE" LOSERS

165. **Jumbles:** COUPLE BALLAD PACKET GAINED FORGOT TAMPER
Answer: An evening dress is sometimes designed to help the wearer catch this—A MAN—OR A COLD

166. **Jumbles:** HUNTER FICKLE WISELY CONVOY PERMIT TEACUP
Answer: When did a dozen swimmers take the plunge—AT THE STROKE OF TWELVE

167. **Jumbles:** PENCIL MOBILE TARGET ORATOR CHUBBY FEDORA
Answer: A cat ate cheese and waited for the mouse with this—"BAITED BREATH"

168. **Jumbles:** ANSWER FEMALE MORGUE ECZEMA PROFIT GADFLY
Answer: What they called the alligator who strolled into the hotel lobby—A "LOUNGE LIZARD"

169. **Jumbles:** ENGINE BISHOP ASTHMA OXYGEN DUPLEX FACILE
Answer: When the lumberjack went into town for supplies, he put a new ax on this—HIS "CHOPPING" LIST

170. **Jumbles:** PARDON ARMORY BROKEN EMBRYO CLAUSE GOITER
Answer: What presidential "timber" is often composed of—MOSTLY "BARK"

171. **Jumbles:** FICKLE SYSTEM PURSUE ORIOLE IMMUNE EXHALE
Answer: To be an expert mechanic requires—FINE MOTOR SKILLS

172. **Jumbles:** BROKER HELMET SWAMPY DECENT ACTUAL EYELID
Answer: The puzzle-calendar factory was still profitable, but its—DAYS WERE NUMBERED

173. **Jumbles:** HUBCAP TALLER DUPLEX HOURLY PURITY KERNEL
Answer: The firsts profits they made from maple syrup were a—DROP IN THE BUCKET

174. **Jumbles:** HUNGRY INHALE YONDER PEDDLE SLUDGE WOBBLE
Answer: He purchased the land to build the skyscraper because he wanted to—BUY LOW, SELL HIGH

175. **Jumbles:** OUTWIT FAIRLY DEFACE WALRUS PURELY GLITCH
Answer: After being dealt a royal flush, the poker player had a—GREAT DEAL OF CHIPS

176. **Jumbles:** KNIGHT ATTEND SMOOCH GLADLY HOTTER EASILY
Answer: When the whole family got involved in building an outdoor living space, it was—ALL HANDS ON DECK

177. **Jumbles:** LEVITY TOMATO MAYHEM SIDING ZIPPER SCARCE
Answer: When the elephant developed a skin problem, they brought in a—"PACHYDERMATOLOGIST"

178. **Jumbles:** OUTAGE DEPUTY FAÇADE SPRING AFLOAT UNFAIR
Answer: With the audience in a circle, the performer received a—ROUND OF APPLAUSE

179. **Jumbles:** EXCESS GOSSIP GROOVY VOYAGE VERSUS VANISH
Answer: The quarterbacks who didn't get along were—PASSIVE AGGRESSIVE

180. **Jumbles:** FATHER HOBNOB ENCORE PICKET GUTTER INFUSE
Answer: The performer earned some money as a mime, but it was—NOTHING TO SPEAK OF